Praise for Advance Your Emergency Department

"In their new book, *Advance Your Emergency Department: Leading in a New Era*, the authors argue persuasively that a patient's experience in the Emergency Department is critical to a hospital's overall performance, and they delineate the key principles required to create and sustain a high-functioning ED in today's challenging healthcare environment. The book's chapters are chock-full of specific, evidence-based tools and tactics for improving operational efficiency, communication, collaboration, and accountability—all conveyed in readily accessible prose, with plenty of real-world examples. This book is a must-read for all departmental and organizational leaders."

—Josh Kosowsky, MD

Clinical Director, Department of Emergency Medicine, Brigham and Women's Hospital, Boston, MA

Assistant Professor, Harvard Medical School

Author of *When Doctors Don't Listen: How to Prevent Misdiagnosis and Unnecessary Tests* (available in print January 2013, Saint Martin's Press)

"If you want a 'world-clais is the book to read. A 'how-to appr ided on evidence-based methods. St e and practi-

cal approach come alive in each chapter—a step-by-step method for creating an excellent ED service. The hospital industry is fortunate to have such an outstanding leader. Thank you, Stephanie."
—Mary Ann Barnes
Senior Vice President and Executive Director, Kaiser Foundation Health Plan and Hospitals

"With this book, Quint Studer and his team of professionals have taken their management tools for the Emergency Department and moved them to the next level of excellence. In these challenging times of healthcare reform, we all find it more and more difficult to connect the dots to CMS requirements and bedside care of the patient. This book helps clinicians ground the concepts and have hands-on learning to the practice of medicine. It helps us focus on what matters most: delivering the highest quality of care to our patients. I have personally worked with each of these authors and can testify to their expertise and knowledge on moving you and your organization to the highest levels of excellence."
—Rebecca Parker, MD, FACEP
Executive Vice President, EmCare North Division

"*Advance Your Emergency Department: Leading in a New Era* provides a roadmap on how to take the Emergency Department from good to great. Regina Shupe, our Studer coach, has shown us firsthand how these practical approaches can improve outcomes in all the pillars of the Emergency Department's operations.

"I highly recommend this book for not just ED leaders, but for all who are responsible for driving flow and operational excellence. The ED is the gateway to the hospital, and it's important we are all aligned focusing on the customer."
—Steve Kishel
Senior Director Performance Improvement, Kaleida Health

"Doing the right things and doing those things right. You may know the right things to do, but are you implementing them correctly? This book shows you the tactics and truly guides you through setting up the foundational skills needed to provide consistent quality care for every patient every time. *Advance Your Emergency Department* is an excellent read. It is specifically geared to us in the Emergency Department and brings it back to why we do what we do."
—Alson S. Inaba, MD
Division Head of Pediatric Emergency Medicine, Kapi'olani Medical Center for Women & Children
Associate Professor of Pediatrics, University of Hawaii, John A. Burns School of Medicine

"I found *Advance Your Emergency Department: Leading in a New Era* to be a very thoughtful roadmap for taking improvement to the next level. Stephanie, Regina, and Dan are experts at leading improvement on all challenges facing the ED. Improving the patient experience, patient flow, and patient outcomes is a manageable process when we approach the challenge with the right resources. This is a valuable resource for our ED and hospital leaders who aren't satisfied with a 'good' department. If you are ready to make the move to 'great,' now is the time to lead the change!"
—Jeff Wood
Vice President of Hospital-Based Services, TeamHealth

"They are there when you need them the most—the Emergency Department. How do you maximize the ED patient experience in today's overcrowded EDs, where a delay can be life threatening? Stephanie Baker's engaging and informative *Advance Your Emergency Department: Leading in a New Era* is a must-read for everyone wanting to improve ED outcomes and exceed patient expectations. In an easy-to-read and informative format, it describes the tools needed to provide the highest quality ED care to every patient every time. Every hospital and every Emergency Department that

strives for excellence should make Stephanie's book required reading."
—Paul Bernstein, MD, FACS
Physician Executive Leader and Author of the Award-Winning Novels *Courage to Heal* and *Flashblind*

"An essential read for anyone interested in emergency medicine. Utilizing field-tested Studer Group principles, insights, and case studies, Ms. Baker outlines methods for improving outcomes in patient care, service, and satisfaction. *Advance Your Emergency Department* is a practical playbook for addressing challenges at hand; for delivering value, quality, and service in today's competitive and ever-changing healthcare environment. The text explains simply and clearly how to 'get it done.'"
—Kirk Jensen, MD, MBA, FACEP
Chief Medical Officer, BestPractices, Inc.
Executive Vice President, EmCare, Inc.
IHI Faculty Member

Advance Your Emergency Department

Leading in a New Era

Stephanie J. Baker, RN, CEN, MBA
Regina Shupe, RN, MSN, CEN
Dan Smith, MD, FACEP

Published by:
Fire Starter Publishing
913 Gulf Breeze Parkway, Suite 6
Gulf Breeze, FL 32561
Phone: 850-934-1099
Fax: 850-934-1384
www.firestarterpublishing.com

ISBN: 978-0-9828503-5-0

Library of Congress Control Number: 2012949789

Printed in the United States of America

To my parents, Saul and Sue, who continually inspire, support, and love me unconditionally in my life journey; to my wonderful sister and best friend, Angela, for her never-ending patience and grace under pressure; to God for His endless mercy and gift of eternal life; and to emergency caregivers everywhere for their commitment to saving lives and restoring health, every patient, every time.

—Stephanie Baker, RN, CEN, MBA

To my husband, Steve, children, Shannon and Bryan, Shannon's husband, Josh, and my grandson, Robert: Your loving support and encouragement has unleashed my spirit and enabled me to follow my dreams and passion to make healthcare better for employees, physicians, and patients. To my parents, who taught me to have a strong faith in myself, and with God all things are possible. To my sisters and best friends, Mary Grace and Dana, who work tirelessly on the front lines of healthcare. You inspire me.

—Regina Shupe, RN, MSN, CEN

To my wife, Kristen, and kids, Emily and Paul: Your unconditional love and ongoing support allow me to pursue my passion in healthcare; to my parents, Jim and Sue: You have lived and supported my healthcare journey from medical school and residency to attending and coach; and most importantly, to God: for giving me health, strength, and forgiveness.

—Dan Smith, MD, FACEP

Table of Contents

Fixing things that seem out of our control

Using a systematic approach

Determining top priorities

Choosing and weighting goals

Tracking results to goals

Forecasting for efficient flow

Diagnosing flow challenges

Three best practices for redesigning flow

Addressing boarding problems in the ED

Using AIDET® for effective communication

Best practices for Hourly Rounding®

Post-visit phone calls: The best four minutes in healthcare

Using simulated skills labs

Taking leader rounding to the next level

Validating with post-visit phone calls

Foreword

Emergency Departments play a vital role, not just inside individual hospitals, not just in healthcare as an industry, but in society at large. We place our trust in them when things get really desperate, when the lives of our loved ones are at stake, when there's simply nowhere else to go.

Now EDs, along with hospitals in general, face an unprecedented set of circumstances. On one hand, the potential for improved outcomes is greater than at any time in history. State-of-the-art technologies and advances in knowledge and skills mean we can do more than ever before to save lives and help patients regain their health.

On the other hand, the cost pressures have never been greater. All areas of healthcare are expected to do more with less, and the demands just keep getting tougher and tougher.

Finally, patients have higher expectations than ever before. Just like customers in all industries, they have come to expect—and have always deserved—prompt, friendly, high-quality service. Crowded EDs and all-day waits are no longer acceptable.

EDs that take all of these factors into account and respond strategically to them have a huge opportunity to shine right now. For many, this will mean renewed attention to financial issues. Yes, it's critical to maintain our laser focus on quality—that almost goes without saying—but it's *just* as critical that all aspects of our work are carried out with a full awareness of the cost side of the equation.

Lately, I've talked a lot about hardwiring profitability. This means making *all* decisions—from how we integrate physicians to how we engage employees to how we communicate with patients—with an eye to using resources wisely, maximizing reimbursement, and promoting growth. Certainly, the ED is no exception.

The advanced strategies and tactics you'll find in this book are meant to help your Emergency Department achieve results more efficiently, effectively, and collaboratively. They help you improve quality and timeliness, of course, but are also inherently designed to help the entire organization maintain and grow its profit margin.

Never have mission and margin been so deeply intertwined. Each allows the other to exist. As we live out our purpose (actually, our *privilege*) of providing lifesaving care to the communities who count on us, we need to be equally passionate about protecting our profitability.

Being able to deliver the highest quality emergency care is great, but it's just a start. It's also critical to do it in a way that ensures our EDs will still be here tomorrow—and that we'll still be able to offer patients the resources, the care providers, and the positive experiences they expect and deserve.

Quint Studer

Introduction:
The New Reality

My, how times have changed in the last 10 years! According to the Centers for Disease Control and Prevention (CDC), Emergency Department visits in the U.S. have increased 37 percent from 1995 to 2010, hitting a new all-time high of over 124 million visits in 2010.[1] That's 222 visits per minute!

Meanwhile, the number of hospital EDs dropped nearly 7 percent[2] (from 4,109 to 3,883). Half of all urban and teaching hospitals are over capacity in their EDs while nearly a quarter of all hospitals (and 45 percent of urban hospitals) spent time on ambulance diversion from March 2009 to March 2010.[3] According to the CDC, ED volumes are expected to increase 5 percent annually for the next five years.

What does overcrowding mean for seriously ill patients? Clinical studies show that it results in delays in lifesaving treatments, poor clinical outcomes, and an increase in mortality rates. (One study showed that patients who waited more than eight hours to be admitted or transferred experienced a 20 to 30 percent increase in mortality rates.)[4]

Other studies show that overcrowding is associated with delays in timely treatment for acute myocardial infarction[5] and community-acquired pneumonia.[6] Delayed admission from the ED to an inpatient bed also increases inpatient length of stay.

Just as EDs are at their breaking point, healthcare reform is creating even more pressure to perform. With the transition to value-based purchasing and the move to more transparency through publicly reported metrics, hospitals are feeling serious pressure from payers, CMS, employers, and patients to deliver a quality experience. In fact, as this new emphasis on performance continues, we'll probably look back in another five years and think that *these* were the "good old days."

The Good News

There's clear evidence that when Emergency Departments improve patient perception of care, inpatient results improve as well, as measured by HCAHPS performance. In the ED, this is no longer a "nice to have" but a financial and organizational imperative.

As the "front door" to the hospital, more than 50 percent of non-obstetric inpatients arrive through the Emergency Department.[7] Because a patient's ED experience provides an important first impression of the hospital, a poor or inconsistent experience is reflected in how patients rate inpatient care, putting critical inpatient reimbursement dollars at risk... one more reason why a consistent, quality experience in the ED is so critical.

Figure i.1

Relationship: ED and HCAHPS "Overall" Percentile Rankings

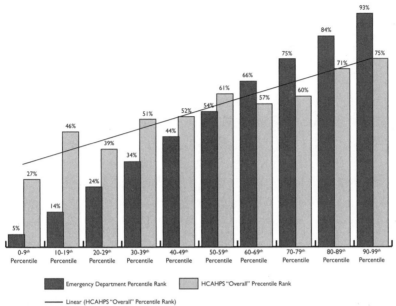

As the front door to the hospital, the ED has a major impact on overall patient perception of care—and therefore Medicare reimbursement—for the
whole hospital. As ED results improve, so do HCAHPS results.

In its 2011 Value Report,[8] the Healthcare Financial Management
Association recommends hospitals can best survive in and respond
to this environment by doing four things: (1) hardwiring a culture
of collaboration, creativity, and accountability; (2) using accurate
quality and financial data to support organizational decision making; (3) ensuring performance improvement by reducing variability
in clinical processes and improving the delivery, cost-effectiveness,
and outcomes of care; and (4) effectively managing risk.

This book gives you the tools to do just that. In Studer Group's
Excellence in the Emergency Department: How to Get Results, we shared
the foundational tactics you need to hardwire excellence, and in
the following nine chapters we'll explain how to operate efficiently,

communicate effectively, and collaborate consistently to take it to the next level. The reality is that what you've done in the past is not going to get you where you need to be in the future. By investing in your development of these next-level skill sets using structure and focus, you *can* build and sustain an agile, high-performing Emergency Department...even during today's tough times.

How to Exceed Patient Expectations

Year after year, surveys show that patient priorities in the ED stay the same. They want to be kept informed about delays, have their pain controlled, and have staff care about them as a person.[9] In fact, whether you provide care in the United States, Canada, or Australia, the top three drivers of patient perception of care in the ED are all the same.

There's clearly no question about what is most important to patients. Surveys also show that ED patient perception of care decreases as wait time and length of stay increases, but that in spite of this, patient perception of care remains high if patients are kept informed about delays.[10]

To meet these expectations in spite of fewer resources and increasing volume, we'll need to hardwire effective behaviors and processes for efficient flow so patients can be diagnosed and treated in spite of these barriers. When we face our flow issues, we reduce patient wait times, improve clinical quality outcomes, and increase patient perception of care. In essence, we create a highly reliable organization.

Consider the path of the patient in your Emergency Department. Each ED visit has a beginning, a middle, and an end. To exceed patient expectations, we need to understand how expectations differ during each phase and hardwire evidence-based tactics to meet and exceed them.

For example, acknowledging patients upon arrival with a prompt, courteous triage is a key expectation at the beginning of the visit. We can respond by expediting the triage process, using immediate bedding to ensure the patient can see the provider as quickly as possible, and implementing Hourly Rounding® in the reception area to keep patients informed while they wait.

In the middle of the visit, patients want to be seen by an ED provider in a timely manner (best practice is 30 minutes or less), be checked on frequently, and feel cared about. They don't want to feel like just a number or a diagnosis. When we use key words, focused Hourly Rounding, bedside report, and leader rounding on patients, we address these priorities.

At the end of the visit, patients want their ED provider to discuss their diagnosis and results and have the opportunity to ask questions. When providers conduct a formal close with key words and conduct post-visit phone calls within 72 hours of the visit, they exceed these expectations. At every stage of the visit, patients want to be kept informed of next steps. It's a critical patient satisfier, and the tactics just discussed address this very well.

A Word about Evidence-Based Leadership℠ Tactics

What's the best way to get results? By standardizing your systems and tools so they are used with every patient every time. Studer Group calls this "Evidence-Based Leadership." It's similar to using evidence-based clinical protocols. By using established best practices, we reduce variance for more consistent quality outcomes. Just as healthcare organizations routinely standardize group purchasing, information technology, human resource policies, and their brand, using Evidence-Based Leadership tactics also creates efficiency.

If some individuals (or some shifts) don't consistently use the tactics that are proven to deliver service and operational excellence in the ED, we'll have a culture of optionality, get variance in our results, and leave results on the table that our organizations just won't capture.

Conversely, when we consistently use Evidence-Based Leadership tools and tactics, we maximize the human potential of each individual to then maximize the organization's potential. The result? A culture of accountability and consistency for a mission-driven, high-reliability organization…one in which employees want to work, physicians want to practice, and patients want to receive care.

When you hardwire the use of these tactics through active training, holding people accountable (no excuses!), and coaching for performance, results can be phenomenal! An engaged workforce is what drives performance. Satilla Regional Medical Center in Waycross, GA, for example, reduced left without being seen (LWBS) patients by .57 percent in one year, capturing an additional 292 patients for $87,600 in recaptured revenue (estimated at $300 per treat-and-release patient).

Six months after Satilla hardwired intensive leader rounding on employees and physicians, their ED overall rating of care by patients jumped from the 19th to 96th percentile. After they began relentlessly Hourly Rounding in the reception area, their patient rating for "how well I was kept informed about delays" skyrocketed from the 13th to the 99th percentile as measured by a large national patient satisfaction database.

First Things First

If you haven't yet read Studer Group's book *Excellence in the Emergency Department: How to Get Results*, begin there. Familiarize yourself particularly with the three "Must Have" tactics in Section 2 to learn how to move your ED results in 90 days. Once you have an in-depth understanding of how to use rounding for outcomes, post-visit phone calls, and bedside shift report, you can move on to the three advanced tactics included in Section 3 of that book: key words at key times, Hourly Rounding with individualized patient care, and interdepartmental communication tools. But remember, you can't cherry-pick it!

In the Emergency Department, sequencing is everything. If the foundational tactics are done well, you can achieve marked improvement. Once those are hardwired, you need to align goals, implement an accountability system (see Chapter 2), and excel at reward and recognition before you will succeed with the advanced tactics featured in this book. They require more team momentum and technical knowledge to really hum, so start with the foundational tactics first.

If your organization has already hardwired the Must Haves® and is looking for ways to drive ED performance further and faster, you're in the right place. Perhaps you are already rounding on patients, but need to do a gap analysis to evaluate how effectively your leaders are coaching and validating staff performance.

Or maybe you've got an effective Split-Flow Model in place, but you haven't yet set criteria and metrics for your Fast Track that everyone follows with every patient every time. Or you're consistently using an expedited triage process, but still wondering how you can get admitted patients out of your ED in a timely fashion.

The following chapters are about advancing operational performance through process improvement, standardization, reducing variance, and accountability. Because just implementing a large number of tactics won't get you where you need to be. It's not only about quantity, but also quality. Compliance and validation—sequenced effectively—are *key*.

In fact, best-in-class EDs hardwire a strong foundation built upon three key principles: (1) operate efficiently, (2) communicate effectively, and (3) collaborate consistently. Just like Studer Group's Healthcare Flywheel®, results build momentum for more results.

Figure i.2
The Foundation of a Best-in-Class Emergency Department

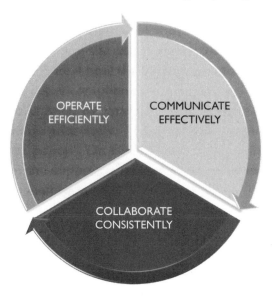

In fact, if you're ready to learn more after reading this book, we encourage you and a few key team members to attend Studer Group's two-day Excellence in the Emergency Department Institute (www.StuderGroup.com/EDI). Recently, we received a note from Joann Ullrich, RN, BSN, and Emergency Department director at Rutherford Regional Health System, who told us how helpful it was to see "real-life demonstrations" on how to handle the situations that occur daily in their units. She felt encouraged by hearing the learning process that each of us as speakers and ED practitioners went through ourselves as we learned, tried new tools, set new expectations, and improved at coaching and closing performance gaps. It's not always a comfortable process, but it is an effective one.

By using these accelerated tools and tactics, you'll equip your ED to respond in this new reality with more efficient flow, improved quality of care, high-performing teams, and less need for service recovery.

It's not magic. World-class Emergency Departments lead, rather than follow. They understand that every patient deserves high-quality emergency care every time in every encounter. They know that they and their staff make a difference every day in the lives of their patients.

It's not a job. It's a calling. And you never know...by putting these tools and tactics in place, the very life you save someday may be your own!

Would You Let *You* Take Care of You?

Recently, at a presentation for over 1,500 leaders, we asked individuals to stand if they had personally been an ED patient or accompanied a loved one to the ED in the last two years.

Several hundred people stood. Then we asked, "How would you rate your experience?" and said, "Please remain standing only if you would return to that ED if offered another option."

And more than a third sat down.

The point is this: Are you running the kind of Emergency Department where you'd feel comfortable and confident being treated as a patient? One where you'd trust staff and leaders with those you love?

If not, take heart! *Now* is our time in the ED. With visits on the rise and reimbursement increasingly linked to providing value in the patient experience, senior leaders are listening. They know that when the ED gets better, their inpatient results are going to improve, which will deliver quality clinical outcomes and improve financial performance. Without fixing challenges in the ED, they can't move the organization. They're ready to hear your solutions.

Yes, we will inevitably have to do more with less. And change is hard, but frankly we're good at change in the ED. Aren't your patients worth it?

To meet our mission in difficult times, we need the right tools. We need to better leverage our ED providers and staff. We need to adopt a "Not on my watch!" attitude where "mandatory" means "always." We need to face our flow issues so that every patient receives timely, quality emergency care every time. And perhaps most importantly, we must be relentlessly committed to saving lives and restoring health.

Read on to get the 21st century training and evidence-based practices you need to drive performance and lead in this new challenging, yet exciting era. Now is our time. Let's shine.

Operate Efficiently

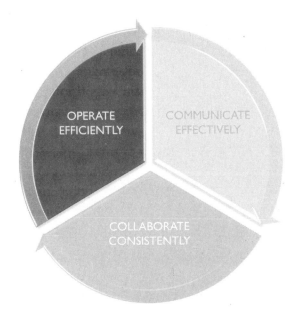

CHAPTER 1

Driving Performance

"Well done is better than well said."
—*Benjamin Franklin*

To drive performance in the Emergency Department, always begin by explaining how the tools and tactics you are asking leaders and staff to use connect back to purpose, worthwhile work, and making a difference. At Studer Group, we put this at the very center of the Healthcare Flywheel. The Flywheel shows how organizations create momentum for change that drives strong results. Our values are at the core of all we do.

Figure 1.1
Healthcare Flywheel® Emergency Department

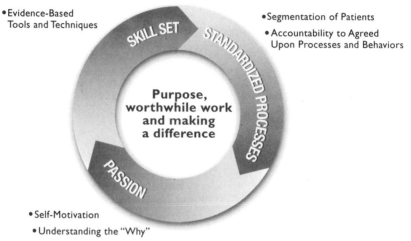

The individuals who work in your ED went into emergency medicine to make a difference in patients' lives. That's why they are willing to deal with the difficult and stressful situations they encounter on a daily basis. In general, they don't lack passion. However, they do frequently suffer from burnout or "change fatigue," particularly when they don't clearly understand the *why* behind a change or process. As you read the following chapters, take note of our own effort to "over-communicate" the *why* as we introduce new tools and tactics. You'll notice that we frequently connect back to the same environmental factors that create urgency for change and the same rewards for implementing change.

While technical and clinical skills are important—and competency is imperative to deliver safe, high-quality care—these qualities must be matched with a high level of patient engagement, communication, empathy, and compassion in order to deliver the best patient experience.

The evidence-based tools and techniques Studer Group recommends in the ED are proven to do just that. Because they are very prescriptive and ensure accountability, they provide the necessary skill sets to deliver consistent outcomes when implemented correctly. A side note: The same rigor must be applied to patient flow processes, so that the right plan is implemented for the right problem, and processes are standardized to reduce variance. We'll discuss that in detail in Chapter 3. Segmenting patients creates efficiency in the ED and leads to better patient outcomes when these standardized processes are applied consistently for patient flow.

Accountability closes the loop. All leaders and staff must know what is expected of them through well-developed and well-defined processes. They must be held accountable for agreed upon processes to reduce variance in outcomes.

In fact, it turns out that many things in the ED are highly predictable. Once we begin tracking, we will know the number of patient arrivals per hour and by day of the week, which then allows us to anticipate by using a methodical, standardized approach that produces reliable, repeatable outcomes. Optionality creates variance, and variance creates risk, so mandatory, agreed upon behaviors must be well articulated and must occur *always.* By first tapping into employees' passion to make a difference, then providing key skill sets to be effective, and finally standardizing processes, we can deliver the kind of care we would want for ourselves and loved ones, every patient every time.

Fixing Things That Seem Out of Our Control

It's clear that we can't do it alone in the Emergency Department. Just as inpatient care needs a positive patient experience in the ED to improve overall patient perception of care, so too do we need to rely on our stakeholder partners to help us deliver a quality care experience in the ED. Nearly 75 percent of ED patients will get some form of lab or x-ray when they come to the ED,[11] so these departments are crucial to our success. Registration, Security, and Housekeeping also keep things running efficiently and impact patient perception of care. In Chapter 7 (Driving Collaboration within the ED), we'll share some best practices for creating efficiency and partnership with these important stakeholders.

However, we also find that when the ED has clearly improved things that are within our control—such as front-end flow—it becomes much easier to enlist the cooperation of senior leaders and other primary stakeholders to address other areas—like back-end flow—that are out of our control. When we take ownership of the areas where we hold influence, other stakeholders are inspired to step up.

Satilla Regional Cuts Average Length of Stay (ALOS) for Admitted Patients by 98 Minutes

"We were frustrated because our ALOS for admitted patients was at 321 minutes," explains Kim Jordan, ED manager at Satilla Regional Medical Center in Waycross, GA. "We knew we needed help from our inpatient team to improve it, so we reached out to senior leaders and formed a multi-disciplinary flow committee.

"The results? The team began using a Situation-Background-Assessment-Recommendations (SBAR) format where the ED reports and faxes to the floor (waiting 10 minutes for questions and sending patients to the floor within 30 minutes); we eliminated black out times for transfer to floors during shift change; we opened a new floor; and we involved Environmental Services to ensure timely cleaning of rooms, especially during peak hours. All of this was a collaborative effort of the ED, the Inpatient team, and Support Services team. As a result, we dropped our ALOS for admitted patients from 321 minutes to 223 minutes: a difference of 98 minutes!"

Use a Systematic Approach to Driving Performance

There are seven key components to effectively driving operational excellence in the ED. It's important to note that they are both interrelated and sequential:

Figure 1.2
Driving Performance in the ED

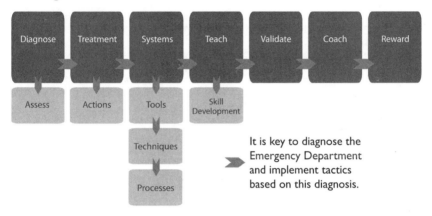

Diagnose

Accurately diagnosing the challenges in your ED is a critical first step to solving them. It's no different from providing quality clinical care. Just as we would never treat a patient before diagnosing them, we should never treat our ED without a diagnostic assessment.

The way to get an accurate diagnosis is to perform a thorough operational assessment of your ED. Your assessment must capture metrics that show how efficient your flow is by reviewing key outcome measures for front-end, middle, and back-end flow. In July 2011, nine prominent healthcare provider associations released a final consensus statement and standardized definitions for key

Emergency Departments.[12] To learn more, read Studer Group's white paper *The Road to Emergency Department Excellence: How the New Standardized Metrics Can Help Us Transform Our Industry*. Download a copy at www.FireStarterPublishing.com/AdvanceYourED.

Here's an example of a few of the most common ED flow metrics that are used, as well as best practices and national averages:

Figure 1.3
Metrics for Diagnosing ED Operational Performance[13]

Metric	Best Practice	National Avg
Front-End Flow		
Arrival-to-triage time	< 5 minutes	10 minutes
Triage completion time	4 minutes	10 minutes
Door-to-provider time	< 30 minutes	47 minutes
Left Without Being Seen (LWBS) rate	< 1 percent	1.9 percent
Middle		
Door to disposition (discharged patients)	< 90 minutes	138 minutes
Door to disposition (admitted patients)	< 180 minutes	248 minutes
Back-End Flow		
Disposition to discharge	< 10 minutes	16 minutes
Disposition to departure (admitted patients)	< 60 minutes	93 minutes

Determine Top Priorities

When you review your ED's current performance on these metrics, ask yourself: What are our biggest challenges? Where is the biggest opportunity for improvement and reduction of bottlenecks? By focusing there first, you will best maximize the impact of the tools and tactics you implement.

The financial impact can be huge! Consider a few examples:

- Decreasing the overall turnaround time in your ED improves patient satisfaction, reduces LWBS patients, and delivers a net gain in virtual beds. In a 36,000 volume ED, reducing turnaround time by 60 minutes—or reducing holding time by one hour per day—would create room for the ED to see an additional 30 patients per day (virtual beds). If half of those 30 patients are realized daily—based on an average ED treat/release visit reimbursement of $300 per patient—this ED would capture an additional $4,500 per day or more than $1.6 million per year.

- When you improve patient perception of care, you improve market share, customer loyalty, and staff and physician satisfaction. Typically, unhappy patients share their bad ED experiences widely. However, if you could grow ED volume by just 1 percent annually (360 patients per year for a 36,000 volume ED) through patient loyalty and positive word of mouth, that would yield $108,000 in additional annual revenue.

- A 4 percent improvement in left without being seen (LWBS) patients in a 36,000 volume per year ED yields an additional 1,440 patients annually for $432,000!

Treatment

Before you start treating those high-priority flow challenges, however, be sure you have set a solid foundation for success with aligned goals (See Chapter 2) and have implemented and hard-wired the foundational Phase I Must Haves:

Figure 1.4
Emergency Department Must Haves®

Phase I: Foundational Must Haves:	Phase II: Advanced Tactics:

• Rounding for Outcomes
   • Leader Rounding on
     Staff and Providers
   • Leader Rounding on
     Patients
 	
 • Post-Visit Phone Calls
	• Hourly Rounding®
	
	 • Bedside Shift Report
	
	 • highmiddlelow®
	
	 • Key Words – AIDET®

Again, as noted in the Introduction, you can't cherry-pick tactics to implement. Sequencing is key. Begin by hardwiring the Phase I foundational Must Haves as prescribed. It's important for leaders to round on staff and providers early because it builds the relationship between supervisors and employees. (Happy employees lead to happy physicians and happy patients.) Leader rounding is the number one action you can take to raise employee, physician, and patient satisfaction. When leaders round on patients, they validate that patients are receiving the best possible care, harvest important reward and recognition, and identify trends and opportunities for improvement.

Post-visit phone calls within 72 hours of discharge save lives! One study in the *Annals of Internal Medicine*[14] found that confusion or misunderstanding about discharge instructions frequently leads to non-compliance with physician discharge orders, particularly around medication administration. (Nineteen percent of discharged patients in the study had adverse events. Of those, 48 percent were preventable!) A follow-up study[15] determined that of those patients who reported adverse events in the original study, 71 percent were significant, 13 percent were serious, and 16 percent were life threatening! (See Chapter 5 for next level tactics for leader rounding and post-visit phone calls.)

Once these Must Haves are hardwired, you're ready for Phase II advanced tactics. Remember, AIDET and key words are not "smile school"! They are about being prescriptive and providing consistent communication in the ED, reducing patient anxiety, and ensuring we provide safe care (just like when we use "Stat!" and "Code Blue!"). We must use words that encourage patients not to leave without treatment. Studer Group calls AIDET (Acknowledge-Introduce-Duration-Explanation-Thank You) the Five Fundamentals of Communication because these key words and actions are so effective at managing patient expectations, increasing compliance, and improving outcomes. You can watch a video of what AIDET in the ED looks like at www.FireStarterPublishing.com/EDAIDET.

Hourly Rounding in the reception area keeps patients informed about delays: a top patient priority at every stage of the ED experience. Bedside shift report is an excellent way to ensure patient safety while building employee ownership, accountability, and efficiency. (Watch a video on bedside shift report in the ED at www.FireStarterPublishing.com/AdvanceYourED.) Highmiddlelow® is a prescriptive approach to ensuring you retain your top employees, develop your middle performers, and hold your low performers accountable with an "up or out!" approach. (See next level tactics in Chapter 4.)

A Word about Getting Results

Remember, breakthrough results come by managing the performance gap. If some individuals or shifts aren't using the tactic with every patient every time, you'll never get the results you're seeking. Again, that's why accountability systems (like dealing with low performers and setting clear, weighted goals on an objective leader evaluation) are so key to making this work. There's a clear correlation: As we consistently meet those top priorities of ED patients—pain, plan of care, and duration—results improve.

The results of your ED assessment will dictate the highest priorities and first actions to take in your treatment plan. For example, if you review your front-door flow metrics and determine door-to-doctor time is 70 minutes (best practice is 30 minutes!) and your LWBS rate is 4 percent, you absolutely need to hardwire immediate bedding to decrease door-to-doctor time and implement Hourly Rounding in the reception area to keep patients informed about delays. (Remember, it's not only clinically unsafe for patients to leave without treatment, but it also puts your organization at medicolegal and EMTALA risk.)

By clearly diagnosing your top priorities for improvement, you can sequence the evidence-based tactics accordingly to make the most impact. (Studer Group coaching includes a comprehensive assessment of ED operations, medical staff, and flow and throughput processes. For more information, see www.StuderGroup.com/Coaching/ED.)

Earlier, we talked about "the path of the patient," or how to take into account patient expectations at each stage of the ED visit. Here are some examples of how patient expectations match up with effective evidence-based tools and tactics—in other words, actions—to treat them, as well as metrics to measure the outcomes:

Figure 1.5

Standardized ED Metric	Patient Expectations	Actions
BEGINNING- UPON PATIENT ARRIVAL ED Arrival Time ED Offload Time ED Transfer of Care from Pre-Hospital Providers Time ED Triage Time ED Treatment Space Time	Acknowledged upon arrival and triaged promptly with courtesy and respect Kept informed of next steps	Expedited triage process Immediate Bedding Hourly Rounding® in reception area
MIDDLE-DURING ED VISIT ED Physician/Advanced Practice Registered Nurse (APRN)/Physician Assistant (PA) Contact Time	Seen by ED provider in a timely manner (best practice is 30 minutes or less) Checked on frequently during the visit- want to be more than just a number Kept informed of next steps	AIDET®/Key Words Hourly Rounding with focus on pain, plan of care and duration (PPD) Bedside Report Leader Rounding on Patients
END- CLOSING THE VISIT ED Documentation of Disposition to Discharge Time ED Decision to Admit Time Admission Time ED Departure Time	Discuss results and diagnosis with ED provider Be able to ask questions Kept informed of next steps	ED provider conducts formal close with patient using AIDET and Key Words Post-Visit Call within 48 hours after the visit

Systems

By putting systems—standardized tools, techniques, and processes—in place, you will hardwire accountability to improve results and reduce variance in behaviors. For example, if you've decided to implement Hourly Rounding in the reception area in your treatment plan, you'll need to make sure staff are well trained on who will do it, how to do it, and what the process is. They'll need to use an Hourly Rounding log, so leaders can track if this behavior is actually occurring consistently.

In the same way, if you are using immediate bedding (also known as "pull until full," where patients are moved to beds right away as beds become available) to improve flow efficiency, you'll need to have a process in place to ensure it occurs 24/7. When you put a patient in a bed, clearly define how the triage nurse will notify the primary nurse and physician that a patient is in that bed and waiting to be triaged.

You'll also need to identify clear, written metrics to measure goals. For example, if you are going to implement immediate bedding, how will you measure and share results daily to ensure you are trending to goal? By reviewing your door-to-bed times daily or weekly, you'll be able to track your effectiveness.

Teach

Teaching skills effectively is critical to performing behaviors correctly. If you are going to ask a nurse to round hourly in the treatment area, she needs to be competent at executing the agreed upon behaviors that respond to those top ED patient priorities we discussed earlier (PPD).

In 2006, the Studer Alliance for Healthcare Research study[16] showed that when these behaviors were consistently executed in the ED, fewer patients left without being seen and against medical advice, fewer families and patients approached the nursing station, and so much more. But if your staff haven't been taught these key behaviors to use during Hourly Rounding and instead round by just "touching base" with each patient and telling them, "It'll be a little while longer," you will never achieve these kinds of results.

Validate

Whichever tools, techniques, and processes you put in place and train on, you need to validate staff competency. Validation is essentially the demonstration of skill competency. So often leaders "think" staff are doing the behaviors, but it is only when we "trust but verify" that we actually validate skills, quality, and consistency of the expected behaviors. You can validate through direct observation, by using a competency checklist, and by using "skills labs." Each of these will be discussed in detail in Chapter 5 on validation and verification techniques.

Coach

Once you have identified the problem, designed a treatment plan, put in place systems for accountability, trained and validated that expected behaviors are occurring, it's time for leaders to coach staff to higher performance.

Some examples: After you've observed the charge nurse doing leader rounds on patients and monitored that her logs are being completed daily, you'll want to compliment her specifically about the things she did very well, and also be prescriptive about opportunities for improvement.

If you've monitored how nurses are doing with rounding in the reception area and bedside triage through direct observation, you may also want to do some leader rounding on patients and ask: "Were you given an update in the reception area while you were waiting? Were you triaged right away when you were brought to the bed?" Once you've collected this objective information, you can recognize successes, share opportunities noted, and coach for improvement. Then, at the daily huddle, you can feed real-time information back to the group to further reinforce the expected behaviors.

Reward

You'll notice in the coaching examples above that we recommended not only being prescriptive about opportunities for improvement, but also being very specific in complimenting staff both individually and in groups about things they are doing well. It's also helpful when leaders are rounding to ask patients if they have someone they would like to recognize and to obtain specific examples of actions that they appreciated. This allows the leader to provide staff with real-time specific feedback that usually supports the expected behaviors. Remember, what gets recognized gets repeated! This is how you build momentum to turn the flywheel of staff engagement.

Three Things to Remember When Making Improvements

1. **Resist the temptation to rationalize poor ED performance.** Many organizations just accept the crowded ED and long patient wait times as the status quo. While there are some variables, we *can* accurately forecast the number of patient arrivals, admissions, and types of patients by doing some simple data mining to proactively reduce bottlenecks in patient flow.

2. **Align organizational goals before implementing tactics.** No ED is an island. Back-ups in the ED create problems that cascade into other departments. That's why shared goals (objective, measurable, and weighted goals that are tied to a leader's performance evaluation and compensation) are so crucial.

3. **Remember that less is more.** Too many EDs find themselves overwhelmed by numerous tactics that individually produce minimal impact. Remember to focus your efforts on identifying and designing a treatment plan for just one or two hard-hitting priority goals.

In Chapter 2, we'll cover all three of these topics in detail.

The Payoff

Once you train, implement, and coach for results, you should see positive trending in the metric that defines success for that challenge. If you get only incremental results, you'll need to go back and review the process (Is it prescriptive enough?) and the quality of execution (Is everyone doing it as prescribed with every patient every time?).

Breakthrough results come with managing the performance gap—setting clear expectations, training staff, coaching for performance, using skills validation, and implementing highmiddlelow performance conversations to further reduce variance and improve the ability to collaborate consistently and hardwire your culture. By aligning and standardizing processes, you engage in continuous process improvement that helps further reduce variance and create reliable, repeatable, and sustainable results to demonstrate a clear return on investment and a high-reliability organization. Any ED challenge can be solved by using the Evidence-Based Leadership framework.

As Darrell Brackett, EMT-PT, MBA, and director of the Emergency Department at Parkwest Medical Center in Knoxville, TN, explains, "By aligning our goals, collaboration, and must-have behaviors organization-wide, we developed leadership that delivers consistent, high-quality clinical outcomes for patients. Not only did we reduce admission cycle time by 32 percent for the 48,000 patients we see annually in our ED, but we improved our virtual capacity with SuperTrack by 18 percent for low-acuity patients and jumped to the 99th percentile for patient satisfaction."

Interested in learning more? Let's talk next about how to align those goals and metrics. Then we'll move on to flow strategies (including SuperTrack) in Chapter 3.

Key Learning Points: Driving Performance

1. To drive performance, always connect back to purpose, worthwhile work, and making a difference to engage leaders and staff. It's the reason they went into emergency medicine. Review the Healthcare Flywheel to understand how passion builds motivation to develop skill sets with evidence-based tools for standardized processes that deliver accountability for results.

2. Use a Diagnose-Treatment-Systems-Teach-Validate-Coach-Reward approach to effectively fix front-end, middle, and back-end ED flow challenges. To get the greatest impact quickly, look for the biggest priorities for improvement first: those that remove bottlenecks. Review key performance metrics; match them to the right tactic, and hardwire relentlessly!

3. Hardwire the Must Haves first. Before you can effectively treat high-priority flow challenges, you must have set a solid foundation by implementing the Phase I foundational Must Haves (Rounding for Outcomes and Post-Visit Phone Calls). If you aren't familiar with these tactics, read Studer Group's *Excellence in the Emergency Department: How to Get Results*. (Order it or download free tools at www.FireStarterPublishing.com/ExcellenceinED)

4. Breakthrough results come by managing the performance gap. Behaviors must occur always, with every patient every time. Reduce variance by coaching for performance, using skills validation, and hardwiring a culture of excellence with highmiddlelow performance conversations.

5. Any ED challenge can be solved by using the Evidence-Based Leadership framework.

CHAPTER 2

Aligning Goals and Metrics

"What you get by achieving your goals is not as important as what you become by achieving your goals."
—Zig Ziglar

When we travel the country coaching Emergency Departments, one of the most frequent questions ED leaders ask is, "How can I get people to do what I need them to do?"

In response, we take a look at their annual evaluation goals. And therein lies the problem. Their goals are often not aligned to achieving key ED and organizational outcomes. As a result, many ED leaders are not carrying enough weight on the goals to create the urgency needed to improve performance. Essentially, they don't have enough skin in the game! We often find that with their current evaluation system, whether or not they achieve those ED goals will make no difference on their annual performance evaluation.

If you want to create urgency to get results in your ED, develop objective, weighted, and measurable goals that align horizontally and vertically throughout the ED and the entire organization. In other words, if your priority goal is to reduce median time from ED arrival to discharge, both the ED medical director and nurse leader must share that same goal—and it should be heavily weighted for both—on their annual leader evaluations. Other ED stakeholders who can impact that goal (e.g., Lab and Radiology leaders) should also carry that goal on their evaluations for the year to create synergy. That's horizontal alignment.

You also need to cascade goals "vertically." The goals of the ED leader must align to those of senior leaders and the CEO of the organization. Likewise, the goals of the ED leader should cascade down to other leaders and staff in the ED to drive urgency and accountability with the entire team responsible for achieving results.

Figure 2.1

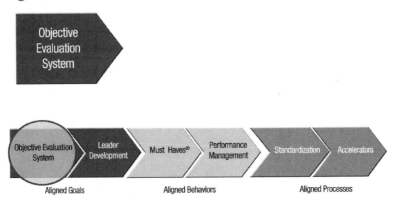

An objective evaluation is the most important Must Have. By aligning goals, you align behavior and processes for results.

Sample Goals

Typically, leaders and staff at organizations we work with have just five to seven goals that fall under the Five Pillars: People (e.g., increase employee satisfaction), Service (e.g., increase overall ED patient satisfaction and HCAHPS overall perception of care), Quality (e.g., decrease wait time, reduce LWBS patients), Finance (e.g., manage expense budget), and Growth (e.g., increase ED volume or market share). This focuses effort for a balanced but large organizational impact.

While the goals must be aligned in the way they cascade, they may be weighted differently according to the level of control and/or influence that particular leader or employee has in reaching that goal.

Here are some sample goals that both an ED nurse manager and medical director might share:

Figure 2.2
Sample ED Evaluation Goals

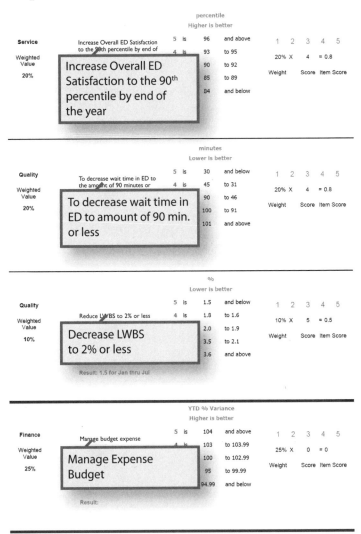

Ideally, these goals would then be cascaded down to assistant nurse managers and individual physicians with certain modifications. For example, if your ED has patient satisfaction data on individual physicians, goals for physicians would differ according to their current performance.

When setting goals, your hypothesis is that the goals you set are attainable. If one physician is already performing at the 75th percentile, it may be reasonable to set a goal to reach the 90th percentile. If another is at the 25th percentile, reaching the 50th percentile is a more reasonable expectation. When reviewing the goals as a group, you want to be confident you can hit the roll-up goal for the ED and the organization.

We also recommend you use a 1 to 5 rating scale in order to clearly delineate levels of performance. A level 3 indicates that an individual is meeting the goal you want to achieve this year; a 2 is a baseline range from last year's performance; and a level 1 would indicate no improvement over baseline. Conversely, a level 4 would indicate the individual is exceeding the expected goal (usually by 5 to 10 percent), and a level 5 would reflect exceptional or outstanding performance. (For more information on setting goals and using Studer Group's web-based Leader Evaluation Manager™, visit www.StuderGroup.com/LEM.)

In short, you want everyone with a potential impact on the goal to be a clear stakeholder. The nurse manager can't be the only one who is responsible for employee satisfaction. Assistant nurse managers and clinical coordinators need to carry this goal as well since they may be the individuals who are rounding on staff and performing the prescriptive behaviors that will improve employee satisfaction.

Be sure to include ancillary departments. If a key goal is to improve turnaround times for Radiology or Lab, then those stakeholders need to carry that goal as well. Again, stakeholdership is both horizontal and vertical. You want to ensure these goals flow both broadly and deeply so you have enough bench strength to get the work done every day to achieve them.

Here's a typical example of a problem we see in goals that are poorly cascading horizontally: In one organization, the board asked the most senior physician leader to improve overall physician satisfaction based on their poor physician engagement composite on their satisfaction survey. This leader's evaluation was weighted at 20 percent, but she failed to cascade that goal to the two physician leaders who had the most opportunity to improve their results, one of which was the ED medical director. This put the organization at serious risk for not meeting this goal. By adding a measurable, specific goal to both of these individuals' annual evaluations—and weighting it heavily at 30 percent for both—they moved results aggressively.

In the same way, cascading goals horizontally is critical. If you're going to give an ED nurse leader a goal to improve a core measure—like administering antibiotics in less than six hours—Pharmacy personnel needs to carry that goal also. When setting goals, ask: Is there enough interdependence to move results?

Choose and Weight Goals

Back in Chapter 1, we emphasized the importance of implementing tactics that address high-priority goals in the ED…those one or two metrics you absolutely need to improve. When setting goals on leader and staff evaluations, be sure they are weighted accordingly.

For example, if an ED diagnoses its biggest challenges as a slow door-to-doctor time and a high number of LWBS patients, those high-priority goals will be heavily weighted on the evaluations of the leaders and staff who can most impact them. While these individuals will still have other goals (e.g., increasing employee satisfaction and managing their budgets), the former goals will comprise a greater portion of their evaluations. This ensures they will focus their efforts on tactics that the ED is implementing to move those metrics (e.g., immediate bedding, AIDET, expedited triage, or Hourly Rounding in the reception area).

Tip: If it's a high-priority goal, weight it at 30 percent or more.

If the nurse manager and medical director have their priority goals weighted heavily, but the assistant nurse managers and physicians who drive those results every day do not, you won't reach the goal. While the weights don't have to be equal as you cascade them down, they still need to be prioritized.

Imagine a nurse manager with a 30 percent weight around a goal who has four clinical coordinators with the goal also weighted at 30 percent of their evaluations. Now imagine a medical director with that same 30 percent weighted goal. She has one assistant medical director who shares the 30 percent weighted goal, but the ED physicians have no weight on the goal. Which leader do you think will be more likely to reach the goal? The nurse manager, of course.

When reviewing the cascading of goals, ask yourself: Am I 90 percent confident that the weights I've assigned are going to deliver the results we're seeking? (This is an important question to answer in advance so that you don't have to use "hope" as a strategy!)

Consider a priority goal (30 percent or more) to be a "non-negotiable" goal. Ensure leaders and staff have at least one on their evaluations. When assigning weights to goals, consider 20 percent a "focus goal" and 10 percent a "maintenance goal."

Also, remember to keep the number of goals manageable. In the example above, if you weighted the LWBS goal at 20 percent and reducing door-to-doc time at 30 percent, that's 50 percent of the evaluation right there. A typical leader will also have goals around improving employee satisfaction, patient satisfaction, and meeting budget. As noted earlier, keep the total number of goals between five and seven so leaders are clear about priorities and don't feel overwhelmed.

Track Results to Goals

If you track results daily, monthly, and quarterly, there will be no surprises at evaluation time. Everyone will have a clear understanding of how they are tracking to goal real-time throughout the year. The best way to achieve that is to use an ED daily and monthly dashboard to review real-time performance.

Develop a Daily Dashboard

By using a daily dashboard at pre-shift huddles (see Chapter 7), you align staff to unit goals, keep staff and providers informed about department progress toward goals and changes, connect staff back to purpose—the "wins" of the work they do—and reward and recognize accomplishments.

While organizations use many variations of a daily dashboard, be sure to include these key items: daily volume, number of LWBS patients, average door-to-doctor time, and average length of stay (LOS) for discharged and admitted patients. Additional process measures may include the compliance rate for Hourly Rounding in the reception area and the post-visit phone call contact rate. Also, be sure that those one or two priority goals you've established appear on the daily dashboard. Here's a sample:

Figure 2.3

ED DAILY METRICS

Date: _____

Week One

	GOALS	MON	TUE	WED	THU	FRI	SAT	SUN	WEEKLY AVERAGE	MONTHLY AVERAGE
PATIENT VISITS									#DIV/0!	
# OF LWBS									#DIV/0!	
% LWBS	< 2% (VHA National Average)		#DIV/0!	#DIV/0!	#DIV/0!	#DIV/0!	#DIV/0!	#DIV/0!	#DIV/0!	
LOS FOR DISCHARGED PATIENTS	< 185 mins (VHA national average)								#DIV/0!	
MEDIAN TIME FROM ED DISPOSITION TO IP ADMISSION	138 mins (VHA national median)								#DIV/0!	
LEADER ROUNDING: % PATIENTS ROUNDING ON	≥25%								#DIV/0!	
HOURLY ROUNDING: % COMPLETE	≥90%								#DIV/0!	
WAITING ROOM ROUNDING: % COMPLETE	≥90%								#DIV/0!	
D/C PHONE CALLS: % ATTEMPTED	100% eligible								#DIV/0!	
% CONNECT	≥60%								#DIV/0!	
MONTHLY OVERALL QUALITY OF CARE PERCENTILE RANK	(Department Goal)									

➡ Patient Rounds: Numerator = Total # patients rounded on by any leader. Denominator= Total daily census

➡ Hourly Rounds: Numerator=Total # of hours in which rounds are documented. Denominator=Total # hours rooms were occupied in 24-hour period. Calculate by multiplying # of rooms by 24 (hours), then subtracting # of hours in which rooms were empty.

➡ Waiting Room: Rounds Numerator= # of hours in which rounds are documented. Denominator=24 (hours)

➡ D/C Calls: Eligible patients are those treated and released to home. Some diagnoses will be excluded.

Download a full-size ED daily dashboard sample at www.FireStarterPublishing.com/AdvanceYourED.

Review the Monthly Dashboard at Stakeholder Meetings

Typically, these meetings include the ED medical director, assistant medical director, the nursing director/manager, permanent charge nurses, a few key staff physicians, and key ancillary and support leaders. It is also important that the senior leaders (those who supervise the stakeholders) attend at least every 90 days to assess results and help remove barriers. Learn more about stakeholder meetings in Studer Group's *Excellence in the Emergency Department: How to Get Results.* (See Chapter 7 in this book to find out about next level tactics to drive results in these meetings.)

Figure 2.4
ED Monthly Dashboard Example

Metric	2012 Goal	Jan	Feb	March
LWBS	<2%	3.1	2.5	1.9
Door-to-doc	<30 min	36	45	30
Door-to-admit time	<240 min	350	305	285
Decision-to-admit time	<120 min	135	115	140
Overall Patient Satisfaction by Date of Service	>75% Pecentile Ranking	61%	64%	78%
Door-to-pain time Renal colic patients	<30 min	47	35	28

Download a full-size ED monthly dashboard sample at www.FireStarter-Publishing.com/AdvanceYourED.

Aligning goals and metrics is the first and most critical step in achieving improved ED performance. Effectively tracking results to goals is the next step. In our experience coaching hundreds of EDs around the country, we find that once leaders establish clear goals and identify how success will be measured—and then train staff and implement the standardized processes and expected behaviors to achieve those goals—results happen.

Also, as results improve, staff feel good about the processes, see value in the behaviors, and adhere tightly to these expectations. This produces even more consistent results, so the flywheel turns with increasing momentum.

Take the time to get this foundational tactic right. Align goals, track metrics that matter, and get staff input on how to improve them. Most importantly, don't apologize for expecting excellence. Our patients' lives depend on it!

Key Learning Points: Aligning Goals and Metrics

1. To create urgency for staff and leaders to get results in the ED, it's critical to develop objective, weighted, and measurable evaluation goals that align horizontally and vertically throughout the ED and the entire organization.

2. Keep the number of goals manageable (no more than five to seven goals) and weight priority goals at least 30 percent of an evaluation for leaders and staff who can have the largest impact. Priority goals are "non-negotiable" goals.

3. Track actual results to goals real-time by developing and sharing daily dashboards at pre-shift huddles and monthly dashboards at stakeholder meetings.

4. Take time to get this foundational tactic right! Aligning goals and metrics is the first and most critical step in improving ED performance. When expectations are clear and measurable, staff feel good about the process and see value in the behaviors, which turns the flywheel for increasing momentum for results.

CHAPTER 3

Driving Efficient Flow

"The best way out is always through."
—*Robert Frost*

Why Is Patient Flow So Important?

Just as establishing an airway is critical during resuscitation, efficient flow is key to achieving and sustaining service and operational excellence in the ED. Increasingly, leaders are recognizing that efficient patient flow is a key driver for quality, safety, and positive patient perception of care. It also allows us to live our mission in the ED by consistently delivering quality clinical care to patients.

In coaching Emergency Departments nationwide, Studer Group finds that unless an ED can optimize flow efficiency, it will continue to struggle in its performance, even if it is communicating effectively and collaborating consistently. In addition to creating important operational efficiencies, good flow is critical for a number of other reasons. Most importantly, bad things happen—sentinel events—when patients who need care for serious illness sit in ED reception areas because there is no treatment space in the ED to begin their care. Patient perception of care also declines as wait times increase.

Figure 3.1
Patient Satisfaction by Time Spent in the Emergency Department

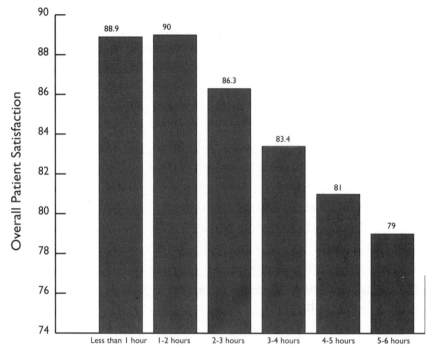

Time Spent in the Emergency Department

Represents the experience of 1,501,672 patients treated at 1,893 hospitals between Jan. 1 and Dec. 31, 2009

Source: Press Ganey *2010 Pulse Report*

Patient perception of care ratings are inversely related to length of stay.[17, 18]

Also, transparency has arrived. At press time, CMS is currently collecting data on three ED throughput metrics and reporting two of them publicly at www.hospitalcompare.hhs.gov:

- NQF 0495: median time from arrival to departure for admitted patients (door-to-admit).
- NQF 0496: median time from arrival to departure for discharged patients (door-to-discharge), (*which is currently collected but not yet posted*).
- NQF 0497: median time from admit decision to departure for admitted patients.

As tougher reimbursement regulations continue to squeeze hospitals, we have a unique opportunity in the ED to make a positive financial impact when we improve flow. As noted earlier, when we reduce wait times, we reduce the number of LWBS patients, realizing income from those patients who stay to receive care instead of going elsewhere.

However, perhaps the most important reason to care about efficient patient flow is because poor flow creates missed clinical opportunities when care is not timely. As providers, we lose the opportunity to administer time-sensitive clinical processes and treatments for serious illnesses like acute myocardial infarctions (e.g., reducing door-to-balloon time to less than 90 minutes), sepsis (early resuscitation, optimization, and antibiotic administration), and stroke (e.g., pharmacologic and catheter-directed therapies for those eligible).

How to Keep Flow Efficient

- Recognize that flow patterns are predictable. Staffing and physical plant space is known.
- Keep vertical patients vertical and moving.
- Have caretakers at each point in the transition.
- Diagnose flow challenges before you try to treat them.
- Make collaboration the norm.

You Know You Have a Flow Problem When...

Typically, we find:

- Many "non-value-added" steps in the patient queuing process (e.g., the patient arrives and waits to give name and health issue; sits back down until called to triage; waits to give insurance information; and then waits again until he is finally called to the back).

- Bottlenecks in flow. Because patients aren't triaged efficiently, the ED reception area frequently backs up while physicians wait with no patients to see.

- Low or no availability of beds. Beds may not be allocated correctly (or perhaps your ED is boarding an inordinate number of admits). Remember, the bed is often the most limited resource in an ED!

- The hospital is losing market share even though competitors are growing or people are moving to the area. (Patients will typically tell 10 friends how awful the ED experience was, putting your hospital's reputation at risk... even for service lines outside the ED.)

How will you know where opportunities for improvement in your ED lie? Begin by walking the path of the patient. Then track metrics using a color-coded daily dashboard.

Figure 3.2
ED Dashboard

	Data Resource	BASELINE		QTR	GOAL	MONTHLY	MONTHLY	*National Benchmarks		
		Jan-Aug 2010	Sept-Dec 2010	QI 11	GOAL	April	May Data Pending	Average	Median	Top Quartile
tSystem PERFORMANCE METRICS	Data Resource	Jan-Aug 2010	Sept-Dec 2010	QI 11	GOAL	April	May Data Pending	Average	Median	Top Quartile
DOOR-TO-DOCTOR Admit (Minutes)	tSystem	50	49	49	45	43		53	46	32
DOOR-TO-DOCTOR Discharge (Minutes)	tSystem	48	56	55	45	42		64	58	42
DOOR-TO-DOCTOR All Disposition (Mins)	tSystem	58	50	54	45	43		59	52	37
DOOR-TO-DECISION (Flagged Admit Patients (Mins)	tSystem	178	174	223	180	237		206	173	137
DOOR-TO-DECISION (Flagged) Patients (Mins)	tSystem	202	163	190	180	197		146	156	96
HBI PERFORMANCE METRICS	Data Resource	Jan-Aug 2010	Sept-Dec 2010	QI 11	GOAL	April	May 1-8	Average	Median	Top Quartile
LENGTH OF STAY Admit Patients (Minutes)	HBI Report	435	425	396	350	338	375	321	309	244
LENGTH OF STAY Discharge Patients (Mins)	HBI Report	231	215	218	200	214	177	174	185	142
LWBS (Excludes AMA, Eloped) (Percent)	HBI Report	2.0%	1.9%	2.0%	1.9%	2.3%	1.9%	1.9%	1.8%	0.7%
tSystem PERFORMANCE METRICS	Data Resource	Jan-Aug 2010	Sept-Dec 2010	QI 11	GOAL	April	**May 1-5	Average	Median	Top Quartile
CHARTS NOT LOCKED within 72hrs (number)	tSystem	5	55	127	0	58	149			
CHARTS NOT LOCKED within 72hrs (percent)	tSystem	0.1%	0.3%	2.3%	0%	0.7%	7.2%			
CHARTS NOT CO-SIGNED within 72hrs (number)	tSystem	1	65	161	0	49	169			
CHARTS NOT CO-SIGNED within 72hrs (percent)	tSystem	0.02%	0.3%	2.1%	0%	0.6%	9.2%			
Number of Visits	tSystem	18913	10759	7765		8066	2082			
PERFORMANCE METRICS	Data Resource	QTR 2 2010	QTR 3 2010	QTR 4 2010	GOAL	QTR 1 2011	QTR 2 2011			
PATIENT SATISFACTION (Overall Standard of Care Percentile Rank)	Press Ganey	50	58	64	75	73				

This ED has opportunities for improvement in most flow throughput metrics (metrics in red are below goal), although they've exceeded their goal for door-to-decision time.

Tools for Demand Capacity Management

As you think about how to operate efficiently, communicate effectively, and collaborate consistently with respect to flow, ask: Am I using the most efficient processes? The most effective communication tools? The right people in the right places?

It's important to use processes, communication tools, and people to regulate efficient flow in the ED for smooth, sequential flow. Yes, we get surges of patients in the ED, but as explained in Chapter 2, we can track data to predict when these are likely to occur and staff accordingly. Since we can identify patient arrival patterns and we already know our bed space and staffing capacity, we simply need to align the two for success by adjusting to meet demand. If we fail to staff appropriately to meet demand, we'll experience challenges in providing timely, quality care and poor patient perception of care.

For example, when we look at patterns of patient arrival by hour (demand) for an ED, it follows a predictable pattern. When you chart these arrivals in parallel with provider capacity (typically two to two-and-a-half patients per hour), the mismatches of capacity and demand become clear. This inevitably leads to higher wait times.

Figure 3.3

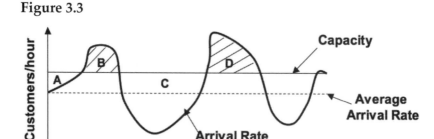

Source: *A Note on Managing Wait Lines* by Professor Edward Anderson, University of Texas at Austin McCombs School of Business

Imagine an ED that is staffed with one provider from 7 a.m. to 10 a.m. At 7 a.m. and 8 a.m., the demand influx is only two patients per hour (well within the safe productivity rate for an ED physician). However, at 9 a.m., the influx pattern shows four patients entering the ED per hour, so the demand exceeds the safe capacity of the provider (one physician). Even if the provider could safely care for these patients' needs, a queue would likely develop with extended door-to-provider times, and at a minimum, communication to patients would suffer. A solution to this flow issue would be to schedule the arrival time of the second provider an hour earlier, at 9 a.m. instead of 10 a.m.

The same phenomenon occurs when nurses are staffed at fixed times (e.g., 7 a.m. or 7 p.m.). Frequently, EDs are overstaffed for part of the morning, but then understaffed for the peak afternoon and evening times. **Always consider variations in demand to layer in staff and providers congruent with this demand.**

Figure 3.4
Average Number of Patients Presenting by Hour

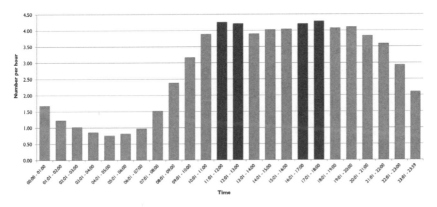

In this ED, volumes are low in the early morning hours but peak between 11 a.m. and 1 p.m. and again between 5 p.m. and 7 p.m. in the afternoon. To reduce wait times, leaders need to ensure staffing is adequate to meet these high-capacity times.

Also, as you consider how to improve flow, **it's critical to accurately triage patients using a credible triage scoring system like ESI (Emergency Severity Index), CTAS (Canadian Triage and Acuity Scale), or ATS (Australian Triage System).** This will help appropriately segment patients and ensure the right patient is at the right place with the right resources at the right time. **The endpoint: Get the patient and the provider together as quickly as possible.**

Patient Transit Simplified: Three Throughput Segments

Essentially, we can break down patient transit in the ED into three key segments: front-end flow (door-to-bed), middle flow (bed-to-disposition), and back-end flow (disposition-to-discharge or admit.) Consider each as a precious throughput segment with dedicated resources to make processes, communication, and people efficient in patient care.

Key Considerations in Redesigning Flow

Whichever model you choose, you'll want to keep in mind these key tenets of designing efficient throughput flow processes:

- ED real estate is precious. Since we have a defined amount of physical space, we need to utilize it in the most efficient way for patient throughput.
- Keep vertical patients vertical! Since we have a limited number of beds, it's critical to design flow processes that maximize their use for patients who most need them. This vertical model is a paradigm shift from the traditional model of care where all patients receive and remain in a bed.
- Use ED spaces only for active care management. This ensures we are allocating our precious real estate and provider resources for the newest or sickest patients.
- Each transit in the ED must have people and processes dedicated to meet the demand. Otherwise, you'll experience bottlenecks.

Hone in first on your biggest areas of opportunity for improvement in each of these three throughput segments by examining the metrics in your dashboard as explained earlier. Then ask key questions to diagnose where the problem lies:

Figure 3.5

Type of Flow Challenge	Ask:
Front-End Issues	• Is triage efficient? • Is patient immediately bedded if a bed is open? • Does the provider see the patient quickly after they are bedded? • Does the ED have open beds to place patients?
Middle Issues	• Is the unit clerk able to enter orders in a timely way? • Is the computerized physician order entry (CPOE) system user-friendly and timely? • Is the nurse able to execute orders in a timely way? • Do essential services execute in a timely fashion? • Is the doctor able to expedite the disposition? • Do admitting physicians call back in a timely manner?
Back-End Issues	Did these activities happen in a timely way? • ED nurse's report • Inpatient nurse's acceptance of report • Inpatient floor's acceptance of patient Also: • Does an inpatient bed exist to admit? • Does the admitting doctor hold the patient in the ED? • Does the hospital have a pre-diversion plan? • Does the hospital have a high-capacity protocol?

How to Redesign Flow: Three Best Practice Models

Depending on the extent and type of flow challenge you identify after diagnosing the problem and reviewing the data, Studer Group recommends you consider these three models to accelerate flow in your ED: (1) Provider in Triage (PIT), (2) SuperTrack, and/ or (3) Split-Flow Model.

While PIT will cater to patients with lowest acuity and need for fewest resources, SuperTrack will address low- to mid-acuity patients with dedicated services and space. A Split-Flow Model is a broader, more comprehensive solution that will increase flow efficiency by addressing the needs of a broader cohort (ESI 2 to 5). Because we find that so many EDs are struggling to meet the 24/7 demands of surges of patients of all acuity levels, we'll devote more space in this chapter to sharing details about the Split-Flow Model that effectively addresses this challenge.

Remember, every ED has unique flow opportunities and nuances. How will you know which system to choose? As we coach EDs nationwide, we begin by diagnosing the specific challenges before recommending a treatment plan. The diagnosis consists of two parts: reviewing throughput metrics and examining actual under and overutilization through a tabletop exercise.

First consider these metrics:
- Percentage of LWBS patients.
- Average length of stay.
- The percentage of patients in each level of acuity group.

Figure 3.6

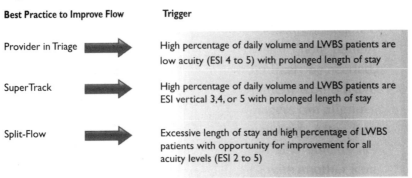

Best Practice to Improve Flow	Trigger
Provider in Triage	High percentage of daily volume and LWBS patients are low acuity (ESI 4 to 5) with prolonged length of stay
SuperTrack	High percentage of daily volume and LWBS patients are ESI vertical 3,4, or 5 with prolonged length of stay
Split-Flow	Excessive length of stay and high percentage of LWBS patients with opportunity for improvement for all acuity levels (ESI 2 to 5)

Understanding where your opportunities to improve specific metrics lie is key. But we also find that conducting a tabletop exercise to examine the current state of flow in the ED provides a valuable real-time opportunity for ED leaders to identify efficiencies and determine which flow model will be most effective in driving performance.

Essentially, Studer Group ED experts coach leaders through an exercise that "compresses" a 24-hour time period of actual patients seen in the ED into a four-hour period and then review the results. It looks something like this:

Figure 3.7

Studer Group's coach Dr. Dan Smith leads a team through a tabletop exercise to examine actual ED flow with real patients.

To watch a webinar of Studer Group coaching an ED team through a real tabletop exercise in progress, log on to www.StuderGroup.com/HealthEastEDFlow. (For more information about Studer Group's ED assessment process, contact 850-934-1099.)

Model 1: Provider in Triage

If your ED has a high number of LWBS patients who tend to present with low-acuity complaints (such as coughs and colds), re-designing your flow process may be as simple as placing a provider in triage. A typical scenario: Your ED is filled to capacity with patients waiting in the reception area while physicians and mid-level providers have no patients to see in back as the ED beds are all occupied with higher-acuity patients.

Frequently, it's low-acuity patients like the ones in the above scenario who leave without being seen. They're not sick enough to want to wait. By physically placing a provider in the triage area to give a quick exam and write prescriptions, you move them in and out of the ED quickly for happier patients, happier providers, and fulfillment of our mission to provide timely care for those in need.

The benefits of this approach are that you'll reduce the high number of low-acuity patients who leave without being seen and increase provider productivity as noted above. You don't need to make major changes to the physical ED space either. You need only a physician, nurse, some basic tools, and a small workspace in or near triage for speaking privately with patients. Some EDs don't even need a dedicated provider at triage. They may just transition a provider up front during a surge in low-acuity patients. Others—who track and can therefore predict surges—may assign a dedicated provider during certain shifts.

The only drawback to using Provider in Triage is that you may end up diverting some patients back to the reception area if your assessment determines they need labs, tests, or more time and resources than you originally anticipated. Yet, most patients are comfortable with this option since they have seen the provider and know what to expect next.

Model 2: SuperTrack

Emergency Departments that can benefit from a SuperTrack typically experience a surge of low- to middle-acuity patients at known times so they dedicate providers and beds during those periods of time.

What's the difference between a Fast Track and a SuperTrack? While both have a dedicated nurse, physician, and secretary for streamlined treatment, a SuperTrack has even more dedicated resources—essential services like x-ray and lab—for rapid cycle testing and treatment to serve those mid-level-acuity patients efficiently and allow for a full exam. The result is a reduction in length of stay and improvement in throughput metrics.

To implement a SuperTrack, you'll need your normal Fast Track equipment, a dedicated care area, nurse, and physician/mid-level provider. Of course, the SuperTrack won't be able to fully meet the needs of high-acuity patients, so you risk having to move them to an available core or hallway bed, which may not be immediately available. Also, it's true that a small percentage of patients—those who expect to spend three hours in the ED for that $400 bill they're going to receive—may feel rushed. SuperTrack can be a paradigm shift for such patients. Overall, however, it's an extremely effective solution for improving throughput for low- and mid-acuity patients. Good communication about the process can go a long way to set expectations for this cohort.

Parkwest Reduces Door-to-Doc Time with SuperTrack

"At Parkwest, our low-acuity patients represent about 5 to 15 percent of our daily volume. Super-Track has been one of many successful strategies we've utilized to improve satisfaction and decrease door-to-doc times for those patients. In fact, using SuperTrack and other strategies since December 2011, we've dropped door-to-doc times from 50-plus minutes to as low as 25 minutes."

—Darrell Brackett, EMT-PT, MBA, ED Director
Parkwest Medical Center, Knoxville, TN

Model 3: Split-Flow Model of Care

An ED that can benefit from a Split-Flow (i.e., segmentation flow) Model of Care typically has opportunities for improvement across the dashboard. It's an ED experiencing surges of patients with all acuity levels that create bottlenecks. Typically, there are no core or full-time beds designated to meet these volume surges. (As a recent U.S. General Accounting Office report points out, the primary contributing factor to ED overcrowding is the lack of access to an inpatient bed.[19] Split-Flow eases, but does not alleviate that issue.)

A Split-Flow Model is a vertical care model and evidence-based practice to improve operational efficiency, patient safety, quality, and patient perception of care. As such, a key principle is to keep vertical patients vertical and moving after an initial evaluation. By moving them through care areas, the ED ultimately opens up beds to increase bed turns and decompress the ED.

However, it's a significant process change for staff and providers. In this model, no provider or patient ever "owns" a bed, for example. Beds are used only for active care management. It's also an "anterograde" model of flow, where patients are moving forward, rather than back to a reception area (which can be frustrating for patients who then feel they are back to square one). The use of a "Results Pending" area is also key to the model.

The Split-Flow Model is an effective and comprehensive solution for EDs with multiple flow challenges, but here's the catch: You'll need to get buy-in for this vertical model, which will require a new (or repurposed) dedicated physical space for patients who are waiting for test or lab results, often known as the "Results Pending" area.

Using a flow simulation exercise prior to piloting the process—like the one described later in this chapter—can help gain valuable understanding and buy-in from both staff and providers.

St. Alexius Gets Results with Split-Flow Model

"We approached this with a 'failure is not an option' mindset," explains Keith Hill, director of Emergency and Trauma Services at St. Alexius Medical Center in the greater Chicago area. "We were very clear with staff that we would not be returning to the old way as it was just not effective. We also ensured that the data to track our progress was in front of our team and hospital executives every day to examine failures and recognize successes. Staff need to know on a daily basis what the goals are and be a part of the information flow."

As a result, 12 months after implementing a Split-Flow Model, St. Alexius's ED reduced ALOS from 255 to 184 minutes (a 70-minute reduction per discharged patient) and reduced LWBS enough to create capacity to see an additional 1,500 patients annually. Patient satisfaction with nurses and physicians soared from the 30th to the 70th percentile. These days, staff say they'd never want to return to the old way. In fact, they compete to see how many people they can send to Results Pending!

How the Split-Flow Model Works

Remember, triage is a process, not a place! In this model, the patient's first point of contact will be a nurse who does a "quick look assessment" by asking five simple questions: name, date of birth, allergies, major medical problems, and chief complaint. This quick look assessment should take less than three minutes and is designed to assign the patient an acuity level. While it's quick, it's also performed by a nurse, not a volunteer or registration clerk. (Remember the earlier axiom: "Right patient with right resource at right time.")

This nurse will coordinate with a "flow coordinator" or charge nurse regarding bed assignment in the ED as this individual tracks patient movement and potential candidates for "Results Pending." Also, a dedicated technician will assist the "quick look" triage RN by taking vitals/pulse oximeter, ECG/Accucheck, and transport patients as needed to the back of the ED. Simultaneously, the registration clerk (in tandem with the quick look triage nurse) will do a quick registration.

Triage Don'ts!

- Taking a full history.
- Completing the medication reconciliation form up-front.
- Allowing retrograde flow back to the reception area.
- Allowing a non-clinician as first point of contact with patient.
- Non-usage of available space in the ED.

Next, Segment Patients

Using the Split-Flow Model, the nurse who did the quick look assessment will triage patients and place them in one of two initial care areas: into the rapid treatment area (for ESI vertical 3, 4, and 5 patients) or to a core bed (for ESI 1, 2, and horizontal 3 patients).

Triage to Rapid Treatment and Intake Procedure

These patients typically suffer from low-acuity complaints (e.g., musculoskeletal injuries, simple infections, low operative suspicion abdominal pain, back pain, migraine) and are of low suspicion for admission. Mid-level providers are often utilized here, and the same rules of engagement on using that precious ED real estate apply. In other words, use *every* space for *active* care management only.

The intake and procedure target time is 30 to 60 minutes. When patients go to the back, they receive a secondary assessment from a nurse and completion of the medication reconciliation form. The provider takes a history, performs a physical exam, and orders initial lines, labs, and medications. Following initial assessment requiring a bed, patients are then moved to the Results Pending area, which we will discuss in more detail in a moment.

Triage to Core Area

Patients who are triaged to core beds are sicker patients who need more provider resources and a bed as noted earlier. There are few changes in this area in terms of how ESI level 1, 2, and horizontal 3 patients are typically managed. However, if their clinical status is downgraded to non-emergent and they will likely be discharged, they can be split to Results Pending. An example: A suspected anaphylactic patient arrives mildly hypotensive after a bee sting. With traditional prudent management, these symptoms often resolve and the patient ultimately goes home. With stabilization of his condition, further observation could be done in a Results Pending area.

How Results Pending Works

The Results Pending area is not a "dump zone" or waiting area. Rather, it's an area for patients to complete work-ups/medications with a dedicated nurse and technician. Patients may be waiting on labs or radiology results. Perhaps they have just been given pain medications or antiemetics and need further observation. In all cases, this area allows for more efficient bed turnover—improving the ED's ability to see newly arriving patients more quickly—while the former patients are monitored before discharge.

A flow coordinator position is key to success with this process. This person is essentially an air traffic controller, except he's coordinating patient flow instead of air traffic. He's watching how things are changing in triage and the back of the ED so he can hopefully offer a bed to triage for the next sick patient in the queue. He's also collaborating with the providers and nurses to facilitate prompt test review and check patient status. If a patient, Mrs. Gonzales, just finished some IV fluids in Results Pending for stomach flu, but says she still feels nauseated, the nurse can say, "Let me contact Dr. Jones, Mrs. Gonzales, and we can get more nausea medicine for you."

Since Dr. Jones is Mrs. Gonzales's physician, he'd be monitoring her care as well, but if he happens to be busy when the nurse needs him, the nurse will contact him to obtain the medication order and reassess her in Results Pending.

Here's an example of a Results Pending area:

Figure 3.8

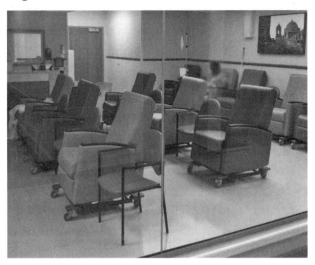

While this is a rather contemporary Results Pending area with a big-screen TV and recliners, the point is to have a dedicated care management area where patients waiting on results are actively monitored by a nurse.

A nurse sits at the desk, near the side of this Results Pending area. Note the small private area at the back of the room in the above photo. This is where the provider can meet privately with patients to discuss their results and treatment plan. If a patient's x-ray shows a broken wrist while he is waiting in Results Pending, for example, the staff can apply the splint right there.

If you triage patients effectively on the front end—so that only vertical ESI 3,4, and 5 patients end up in Results Pending, patient flow will be efficient and patients will receive safe, timely care. Likewise, you must staff Results Pending with a dedicated nurse and technician for clinical oversight and ongoing treatment.

Otherwise, patients will stack up, and their ongoing clinical needs or readiness for discharge can't be adequately addressed.

We also find that because the Results Pending (RP) nurse is a master of the back-end, she can anticipate completion of testing and treatment before the physician can, as she is dedicated to this phase and space of the patient care. Discharges also tend to be executed more quickly as the RP nurse is not receiving acute patients like those in the core area.

How to Find Space for Results Pending

In the earlier photo, this ED had the opportunity to build a new space. However, most Emergency Departments don't have this luxury, so they get creative with existing space and cost-effective solutions. Start by reviewing a map of your current physical space. Then ask yourself: *Since ED real estate is precious and our goal is to maximize the use of space, where do we have space we could convert to a Results Pending area?*

Figure 3.9

This is the Results Pending area at John Peter Smith Health Network in Fort Worth, TX. Imagine this precious real estate as a supply closet a year earlier!

Assessing the Benefits of a Split-Flow Model for Your ED

How much can your ED benefit by adding a Results Pending area in a Split-Flow Model? If your ED has multiple flow challenges for diverse acuity patients, the short answer is usually a great deal.

At John Peter Smith Health Network (JPS), a large academic medical center in Fort Worth, Texas (98,000 ED visits per year), hardwiring a Split-Flow Model resulted in a 35 percent improvement in LWBS and AMA patients over 10 months. On some days, the vertical pathway of Split-Flow actually processes 60 percent of visits in a 24-hour period!

"Like most tertiary care centers, we focus on identifying and implementing best clinical practices to improve care," explains Rick Robinson, MD, FAAEM, FACEP, operations chairman and residency program director in the Department of Emergency Medicine at JPS. "Split-Flow represents an important shift in the delivery of products and services to ED patients. However, success is resource dependent. The single most important resource is the medical and nursing staff ratio."

Baptist Medical Center Gets Results with Split-Flow Model

Baptist Medical Center, a high-acuity Emergency Department affiliated with Baptist Health System in San Antonio, TX, faced operational challenges for years. LWBS rates neared 10 percent; LOS for discharges averaged nearly four hours; and LOS for admits averaged nearly seven hours. Patient satisfaction was often in the lowest quartile of a large national database measuring patient satisfaction.

Four years ago, Baptist's ED Director Gina Grnach—along with executive leaders, a team of ED physicians, nurse managers, and service excellence staff—implemented the Split-Flow Model. The team used LEAN analysis, changed the flow process, remapped the physical plant, and aligned staff and providers.

Six weeks later, Baptist's ED had significantly improved—and has sustained this improvement—in all metrics. In the first quarter of 2012, Baptist ED's LWBS is just 0.5 percent. LOS for both admits and discharges decreased 40 percent in 2011. Equally important, staff and provider satisfaction has increased since implementation because they now work in a service-friendly environment, one that enables them to meet their mission of providing timely, quality care to every patient every time at Baptist. Due to the success of this beta site, Emergency Physicians Affiliates (the medical group that provides ED physician coverage) has deployed the process at other Baptist EDs in San Antonio.

Back-End Blues: How to Address Boarding Problems in the ED

No discussion of flow would be complete without a mention of one of the most significant challenges that EDs face daily nationwide with respect to overcrowding. Several studies point out that the root cause of overcrowding is "boarding" of patients.[20]

This prolific problem involves "holding" admitted or pending-transfer patients in the ED, resulting in further loss of precious bed capacity. In fact, a recent survey of a cross-section of U.S. hospitals found that 73 percent of hospitals admitted to Monday evening boarding of at least two patients.[21] A 2010 American Hospital Association survey[22] revealed that 38 percent of hospital EDs were operating "at" or "over" capacity.

Numerous downstream effects result from the boarding burden, including:

- Loss of capacity to treat the queue of patients who predictably arrive in the ED.
- Longer cycle times for emergency patients.
- Decreased bed turns for the ED.

- Suboptimal quality and safety for boarded patients (because care is provided by ED nurses who are not trained to provide inpatient-level care).
- Poor perception of care and safety by boarded patients who are frequently housed in hallways with lack of privacy.
- Lack of patient confidentiality.

While models like Split-Flow can significantly reduce cycle times and throughput intervals, they do not displace or lessen the gravity of the boarding problem. In fact, in trials of Split-Flow in EDs with boarding challenges (e.g., loss of bed capacity greater than 25 percent), such EDs have achieved only minimal improvements in throughput times due to the lack of available beds and capacity.

To improve service and quality in the ED, hospitals must confront the institutional, systemic problem of boarding to free the ED of the boarding burden. This can be achieved only by development of hospital-wide flow teams with engagement of unit managers, physicians, and executive leaders and use of real-time systems, principles, and processes.

Tactics that address this issue effectively include:

- Deployment of flow coordinators who track hospital-wide flow, including discharges, admits, bed status, and staff capacity (just like air-traffic controllers!).
- Thoughtful scheduling of elective surgeries to eliminate the coupling of high-surgical case days on known high-census ED days (e.g., Mondays).[23]
- Proper placement of patients in the appropriate inpatient setting based on diagnosis, with avoidance of telemetry overuse.
- Early rounding by providers (e.g., by 9 a.m.) and early discharges (e.g., before noon).

- Use of discharge lounges for known discharges who await rides or discharge paperwork.
- Daily bed meetings at key times with key stakeholders to consistently identify available beds and preemptively match staffing to patient census.
- Preemptive, quantitative crowding measure, like NEDOCS (National Emergency Department Overcrowding Score).
- Code purple/full capacity protocols, where ED boarders are moved to inpatient hallways for care or transferred to alternate in-system hospitals that have the capacity to properly care for these patients.

Further resource information related to boarding solutions can be found in the *2008 ACEP Task Force Report on Boarding*.[24] (Or to discuss concerns unique to your ED, contact one of Studer Group's ED coach experts directly at 850-934-1099.)

What is clear is that addressing ED and hospital-wide flow requires a proactive and preemptive approach where leaders and staff collaborate, utilize best practice flow solutions, and employ vigilant 24/7 surveillance. Efficient patient flow requires the efforts of all key stakeholders, and no one unit or person can solve the flow conundrum alone.

Are You Ready?

Our hope is that you feel inspired and ready to fix the flow challenges that plague your ED after reading this far...because you *can*! If you follow the basic tenets of flow as we've outlined here and accurately assess where your bottlenecks and non-value-added steps occur, you can create significant improvements in flow efficiency within your ED.

Some of you may wish to take it to the next level by implementing one of the formal flow models discussed here so staff and patients see the kind of results like those enjoyed by the EDs featured in this chapter.

A final note: It is beyond the scope of this chapter to offer an in-depth treatment of the many useful principles and methodologies that assist in understanding queuing systems, addressing cycle times, and improving demand-capacity management. Please see page 195 for a list of recommended reading organized by area of interest.

For more information on how to maximize many of the tactics included here, watch our free webinar on how to improve flow at www.StuderGroup.com/FlowQA.

Key Learning Points: Driving Efficient Flow

1. Efficient flow is a key driver for quality clinical care, safety, patient perception of care, and financial performance. Unless an ED optimizes flow, it will continue to struggle in its quest to reach organizational and ED goals in all of these areas.

2. Key tenets of efficient flow include the ability to recognize and align to predictable flow patterns, forecast flow to match staffing capacity to demand, and address limitations in physical space. (ED real estate is precious!) It's also important to diagnose flow challenges before treating them, keep vertical patients vertical and moving, have caretakers at each point in the transition, and use ED core spaces only for active care management.

3. Consider using three best practice flow efficiency models: Provider in Triage, SuperTrack, and the Split-Flow Model. All three models require triage of patients by acuity levels using a credible triage scale. Which model you choose will depend upon your ED's mix of acuity patients, percent of LWBS patients, and type of flow challenges.

4. Boarding is a problem that can be fixed only after recognizing its systemic nature. It requires attention and commitment from key stakeholders, ranging from the C-suite to unit managers and physicians. To eliminate the boarding problem and sustain hospital-wide flow, use preemptive processes to identify prospective discharges (e.g., early provider rounding), offer discharge lounges, use an objective bed capacity scoring system, and hardwire frequent daily bed meetings.

Communicate Effectively

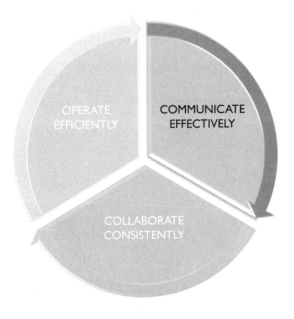

CHAPTER 4

Advanced Communication Tools

"Do not let what you cannot do interfere with what you can do."

—*John Wooden*

There are three advanced must-have tools that improve communication with patients to accelerate results in the ED: (1) AIDET, (2) Hourly Rounding in the ED and reception area, and (3) Post-Visit Phone Calls. While Studer Group considers leader rounding to be a foundational Must Have, we'll also revisit it here and share best practices for taking it to the next level because it's so critical. If you are not familiar with basic implementation of these tactics, please refer to *Excellence in the Emergency Department: How to Get Results.*

In the same way that we coach organizations, let's begin with the reasons *why* we use these tools before we tackle the "what" and the "how." Frequently, in our urgency as leaders to improve results, we are tempted to move to tactical training first, missing that most important motivator: connecting back to purpose. For providers and staff, it's about creating a collegial working and learning environment while delivering great patient care.

By using these evidence-based tools and tactics consistently, we more consistently deliver quality clinical outcomes. These tools also align with top patient priorities. In fact, one study found that for every one-point reduction in satisfaction scores, there is a 6 percent increase in complaints and a 5 percent increase in risk management events![25] (When patients perceive the physician has not listened, demonstrated respect, or provided adequate feedback, they are more likely to take legal action or complain should a suboptimal outcome occur.)

As we educate physicians on effective communication we reduce malpractice risk. In short, we require accountability for using these evidence-based tools and tactics because it creates a "best-in-class environment" for patients, staff, and physicians.

Also, providers sometimes don't realize that in the mind of the patient, their experience is not rated on the quality of the clinical care they receive. Patients have no basis for judging if Dr. Smith made the right diagnosis and prescribed the right treatment. Their confidence in his ability to do that is a "given" if they choose to see him. (Actually, "skill of the physician" is ranked #37 out of 38 in patient priorities in Press Ganey's inpatient patient satisfaction database.)

Instead, patients will rate him on courtesy, compassion, wait times, and comfort care. Communication has become such a priority for providers that the Accreditation Council for Graduate Medical Education (ACGME) requires physicians to demonstrate sufficient interpersonal skills and professionalism during residency training.

"AIDET is like a gift to physicians because it tests and validates ACGME-required core competencies like professionalism, interpersonal/communication skills, and patient-centered care," notes Dr. Rodney Tucker, associate professor and palliative care medical director at the University of Alabama at Birmingham (UAB). As director of UAB's inpatient palliative care programs and associate quality officer for patient experience at this large academic health system, Dr. Tucker has coordinated and supervised the training of more than 800 physicians and providers—including residents—on

AIDET. Increasingly, we see large academic medical centers following his example.

Five Simple Truths about Patient Perception of Care

1. A more satisfied patient means more satisfied staff and physicians.
2. Satisfied patients spread positive word of mouth for higher market share and growth.
3. Patients are more compliant with treatment when they trust physicians and staff.
4. Physicians prefer to work with an engaged staff and organization (and vice versa).
5. Organizations with physician stewardship of this model will thrive and differentiate themselves.

The Power of Our Words

To communicate effectively with patients, we must choose our words carefully. What we say and how we say it has a tremendous impact on our patients. The right words can calm, comfort, and reassure. The wrong words can create anxiety and confusion in a situation that is likely already stressful.

As healthcare providers we owe it to our patients—and ourselves—to *ensure* we communicate in a way that reduces anxiety. Calm, engaged patients are more likely to align with and listen to their healthcare provider for better compliance with their treatment. Research also shows that using key words in triage reduces LWBS patients.[26]

In addition to greater clinical compliance with treatment regimens and fewer lawsuits, physicians who communicate effectively with patients have lower 30-day readmission rates (critical with CMS reimbursement changes as we'll explain below) and higher patient perception of care. Not surprisingly, when patient perception of care improves, *all* quality metrics improve. (There is also a well-established link between patient perception of care and quality.[27])

Clearly, communication also matters in a pay-for-performance environment. Hospital reimbursement depends on how patients answer HCAHPS questions about courtesy and respect, careful listening, how well we kept them informed about treatment, offered understandable explanations, and helpfulness of staff. (At press time, the HCAHPS composite rated third lowest nationally was "Patients always received help as soon as they wanted it.")

Remember, while the HCAHPS survey captures only *inpatient* data now, the patient experience in the ED has a huge impact on how patients rate their hospital stay as noted earlier. In fact, nursing communication is the HCAHPS composite that is most highly correlated with the overall hospital rating.

The words we hear most often are the "words to avoid" below. They have no positive impact on patients' expectation of how long things will take (duration). Even though we may not know, we can more clearly set realistic expectations by explaining, "We are committed to keeping you informed of your progress so we will be rounding hourly to update you," for example.

In the same way, when we say, "Mr. Thomas, I'm giving you this medicine to reduce your pain...*Hopefully*, this will take care of it," we create anxiety. Hope is not a strategy! An alternative statement might be, "Mr. Thomas, I am giving you this medication to reduce your pain. I will recheck you in 20 minutes. If this has not improved your pain to an acceptable range, I will check with the doctor to review your plan and make adjustments." Using words such as *care, concern, safety,* and *privacy* reduce anxiety. Use them often.

Using the word "probably" (e.g., "Ms. Li, we are *probably* going to get an x-ray of your ankle.") is another vague and non-specific word that creates anxiety. We are either going to get an x-ray or not. Instead say, "Ms. Li, we are going to get an x-ray of your ankle, then review and proceed from there with the appropriate treatment for this injury." This instills trust.

Words to avoid also include "try," "pretty good," "pretty quick," "maybe," and "as soon as possible." Instead, use key words that connect the dots for patients on why we are doing certain actions or that address their priorities (PPD). Say, "We care about your pain," or, "Do you have any other concerns?" Explain that you are doing something "to maintain your privacy" or "for your comfort." Explain that "Our next step will be…" or that something will occur "within the next 45 minutes."

Is communicating differently always comfortable for staff and providers? Of course not! But as one of Studer Group's best-selling authors and international healthcare presenters Rich Bluni, RN, frequently reminds us: There is no progress, success, or achievement in life without some level of discomfort. If you want to get in shape, you're going to be sore. If you want to excel at a job, you're going to have to get there early and stay late sometimes.

The same is true for adopting a new communication style. When the evidence demonstrates best practices for communicating effectively with patients, you're going to have to get comfortable with being uncomfortable if you want to be the best at what you do.

Using AIDET for Effective Communication

Increasingly, healthcare leaders who make the connection between the way we communicate and the outcomes achieved are embracing Studer Group's Five Fundamentals of Patient Communication, or "AIDET."

Figure 4.1
Studer Group Five Fundamentals
AIDET® — Emergency Department

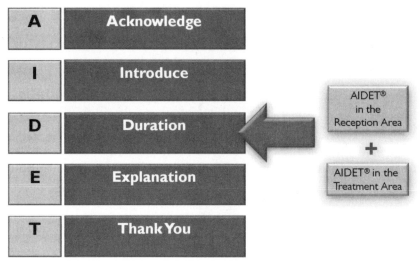

When AIDET® is used prescriptively and consistently in the ED reception area and treatment area, it has a positive impact on patient perception of care.

AIDET® is a communication framework that reduces patient anxiety and improves clinical outcomes. When used in conjunction with Studer Group's Evidence-Based Leadership℠ (EBL) framework, AIDET will increase your likelihood of creating a culture of consistent excellence (a culture of *always*) that meets the tough requirements set forth in healthcare today. If you're not yet familiar with the basics of AIDET, please refer to Chapter 7 in Studer Group's *Excellence in the Emergency Department: How to Get Results.*

As Dr. Harneet Sethi, ED medical director at Cheshire Medical Center/Dartmouth-Hitchcock Keene Emergency Department in Keene, NH, says, "What's most valuable about AIDET is that it provides a concrete framework for high-quality patient interactions. We can train staff in these competencies specifically, instead of just asking them to be nicer."

In a two-year period since the ED introduced AIDET, nurse leader rounding, and bedside report, it dropped LWBS to 1.3 percent, skyrocketed from the 10th to the 96th percentile in patient satisfaction, and realized more than $2 million in a surge of new patients due to higher market share...all while keeping door-to-doc time stable at an impressive 41-minute average.

Nursing Director Cheryl Pinney offers this as her top tip: "Don't give up! This requires persistence and true buy-in from leaders, particularly physicians. It can't be something that only nurses and registration staff do in the ED. We regroup and refocus after a challenging shift. Every patient gives us another opportunity to get it right."

An Example of Effective AIDET in the ED Reception Area

A-Acknowledge: Use engaged body language, which includes making eye contact, smiling, and acknowledging the patient verbally. For example, "Good morning. How are you?"

I-Introduce: "Hello, I am Marta, the registered nurse who will assess you today. So, tell me a little bit about what brings you here today."

D-Duration: "Mrs. James, we are experiencing a high volume of patients in the ED right now. I am going to ask you to take a seat in the reception area. We are committed to keeping you informed of your progress so we will be rounding in the reception area every hour to check on you."

E-Explanation: "Based on what you have told me, I feel you are safe to wait in our reception area. I will be your point person. If you feel your condition changes, please let me know."

T-Thank You: "Thank you for trusting us to care for you, and for your patience while waiting."

Frequently though, we encounter organizations that tell us their physicians and nurses are already using AIDET, but their overall patient perception of care hasn't improved. This is a common experience. The best way to evaluate why AIDET is not effective is for leaders to directly observe staff to assess the quality of the communication provided.

Best Practices for Hourly Rounding in the Emergency Department and ED Reception Area

Why do we round in the ED treatment and reception areas? It allows us to proactively (rather than reactively) respond to patients who are waiting. We can reset expectations by addressing those top drivers of patient perception of care: manage pain, discuss plan of care and duration (PPD), conduct an hourly safety assessment to look for changes, and build trust with the patient by keeping them informed about delays.

We round hourly because of the overwhelming evidence that it offers the highest standard of clinical care for patients waiting to see a provider. In 2006, Studer Group tested the impact of eight rounding behaviors in 32 EDs nationwide. ED nurses used opening key words to introduce their skill set and experience, performed scheduled tasks, addressed PPD, assessed comfort needs, conducted an environmental assessment, used closing key words, explained when someone would return, and documented the round on the log or chart.

Figure 4.2
Eight Behaviors for Hourly Rounds

Hourly Rounding Behavior	Expected Results
Use opening key words	Contributes to trust, therapeutic relationship
Accomplish scheduled tasks	Contributes to efficiency
TOP THREE REASONS FOR CALL LIGHTS Address PPD (pain, plan of care, duration)	Quality indicators and anxiety management– pain control, understanding of care, and explanation of wait times
Address additional comfort needs (warm blanket, pillow, etc.)	Concern and caring, therapeutic relationship
Conduct environmental assessment	Contributes to safety, quality, decreased falls
Ask, "Is there anything else I can do for you before I go? I have time."	Contributes to efficiency Improves teamwork and communication
Tell each patient when you will be back	Contributes to efficiency, is proactive, therapeutic relationship
Document the round	Quality and accountability

To hardwire Hourly Rounding for results, use these eight behaviors with every patient every time.

The study showed that Hourly Rounding reduced LWBS patients by 23.4 percent, AMA patients by 22.6 percent, and falls by 54.5 percent. (In 2009, the CDC reported 0.288 falls per thousand ED patients.[28] That's 14.4 falls per year in a 50,000-volume ED, and many are above this national average!)

In addition, call light usage decreased by 34.7 percent, and the number of families and patients who approached the nursing station decreased by 39.5 percent. Patient satisfaction also increased between 5 and 20 mean points in all areas measured. (You can read the complete results of the 2006 study, which was published online in the *American Journal of Nursing*,[29] at www.FireStarterPublishing.com/AdvanceYourED.)

By hardwiring Hourly Rounding in the reception area as well as Hourly Rounding in the ED, many EDs nationwide are seeing major improvement in these metrics. For example, the Emergency Department at Baylor Regional Medical Center in Grapevine, TX—which sees 50,000 patients annually—reduced LWBS patients from 6 to 2 percent for a return on investment of $480,000 (based on seeing an additional 2,000 patients per year at an average treat-and-release rate of $240 per patient).

Who rounds in the reception area? The triage nurse, charge nurse, lead ED physician, and others appointed by the charge nurse. Rule of thumb: If patient arrival-to-discharge time is less than 150 minutes, rounding should occur every 30 minutes. If it's greater than 150 minutes, rounding should occur hourly.

How can you ensure staff are rounding on every patient every hour? We recommend a "teach-track-validate" approach that we will explain further in Chapter 5. It's also key that managers review the rounding log every shift, rewarding and recognizing behaviors you want to reinforce and specifying opportunities for improvement, both individually and during pre-shift huddles.

Best practice recommendations for reception area rounding include:

- Triage nurse identifies herself as the patient's nurse.
- Mandatory use of the reception area rounding log (download sample templates at www.FireStarterPublishing.com/AdvanceYourED). Determine where log will be kept and clarify goals and expectations for using it.
- The triage nurse owns reception area rounding, but others (e.g., greeter, charge nurse, ED tech) can help.

- Goal is to keep patients informed.
- Keep it simple!

We find that staff frequently struggle with "duration" when rounding hourly just as we mentioned above with respect to AID-ET. Earlier, we offered some suggestions to address those concerns with more prescriptive key words. The important thing is to let patients know that we are committed to keeping them informed about delays in the ED and when we will return. In the ED or reception area, we can let patients know that we will return in an hour or so. This gives us up to 75 minutes and is a time frame expectation we can frequently meet.

Best practice recommendations for Hourly Rounding in the ED include:

- Be sure to role model and role play what the eight behaviors look like.
- Make expectations clear.
- Ensure that the shift charge nurse monitors rounding logs to validate they are complete.

Review results from Hourly Rounding in the reception area and in the treatment areas at daily pre-shift huddles (see Chapter 7) and report results monthly with staff, physicians, and senior leaders. Use individualized one-on-one coaching during monthly sessions with employees if needed. And, of course, reward and recognize without restraint. Visit www.StuderGroup.com/LearningLab to view samples. (This link is available only to Studer Group coaching partners.)

Post-Visit Phone Calls: The Best Four Minutes in Healthcare

If you're not yet familiar with the basics of how and why to make post-visit phone calls, please refer back to *Excellence in the Emergency Department: How to Get Results* (which also includes a sample post-visit phone call template for making the calls and a trend report for tracking the calls). And yes! They take an average of just four minutes each.

In short, post-visit phone calls improve clinical outcomes, reduce preventable readmissions, increase patient perception of care, and most importantly, literally save lives! And yet, it is not unusual to see leaders struggle with staff resistance as they prepare to implement post-visit phone calls.

To reduce resistance, always remember to begin by connecting back to the clinical value of the calls. Post-visit phone calls validate the quality of care delivered in the ED and tell us how well we are hardwiring behaviors for process improvement to deliver better care.

They give us an opportunity to "extend the walls of the hospital" by reconfirming discharge and medication instructions, and verifying scheduled follow-up appointments. By telling the patient before discharge that we'll be calling to check on how they're doing within 24 to 72 hours, we also reduce patient anxiety, which improves compliance, and ultimately impacts whether or not they need to return to the hospital. Consistently, leaders with staff who were very reluctant to begin post-visit phone calls tell us that once their staff began making calls and saw for themselves the tremendous clinical difference they make for patients, they wouldn't stop making them for anything!

Earlier, we talked about the opportunity for ED leaders to get the support and leadership they need from senior leaders in their organizations due to new urgency they're feeling from CMS Medicare reimbursement pressures.

Post-visit phone calls are a timely and highly effective response to reducing the hospital readmissions that will pose a huge financial risk to hospitals starting October 1, 2012 (FY2013). On that date, CMS will reduce Medicare payments up to 1 percent based on a hospital's ratio of actual-to-expected readmissions. In FY2014, the maximum payment reduction climbs to 2 percent, and is capped at 3 percent for FY2015 and beyond.

If you ask most hospitals, you'll find they have calculated what's at risk for value-based purchasing. Far fewer have calculated the risk for preventable readmissions, but we are often seeing hospitals with more than $1 million at risk in FY2012 alone.

So if you're an ED provider, leader, or nurse and are interested in raising the standard of clinical care in your ED, this is actually good news. Considering the dollars at stake in readmissions, the financial return on getting post-visit phone calls hardwired is just too significant for your organization to ignore. Even more importantly, it's critical we verify the patient is recovering safely at home and won't have to return to the hospital.

Figure 4.3
Reduce Readmissions

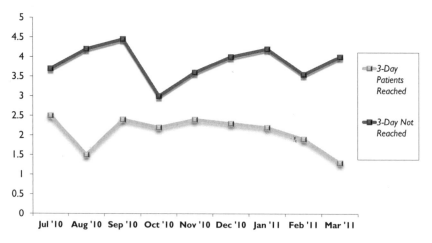

Patients who received a post-visit phone call at this South Carolina academic medical center within 72 hours after discharge had lower readmission rates.

Research shows that when you match good discharge communication with a post-visit call home, the clinical impact for patients is unmatched. In one study, adding a post-visit phone call to well-executed discharge instructions resulted in a 74 percent reduction in 30-day readmissions post-discharge for heart failure patients, an overall readmission rate of just 5 percent, and a 43 percent improvement in patient satisfaction.[30]

If you review the correlation between HCAHPS performance and post-visit phone calls, it's clear that patient perception of care is a byproduct of high quality. Patients who receive calls rate organizations significantly higher on a number of HCAHPS measures, including explanation of new medication, medication side effects, help after discharge, instructions to care for yourself at home, and overall hospital rating.

Figure 4.4

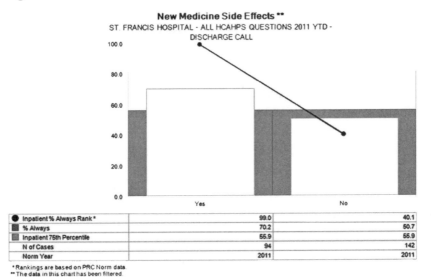

● Inpatient % Always Rank*		99.0	40.1
■ % Always		70.2	50.7
▨ Inpatient 75th Percentile		55.9	55.9
N of Cases		94	142
Norm Year		2011	2011

* Rankings are based on PRC Norm data.
** The data in this chart has been filtered.

At Roper St. Francis Hospital in Charleston, SC, inpatients who received a post-visit phone call ranked in the 99th percentile compared to all hospitals in the database on the HCAHPS question "Always explained possible medication side effects in a way I could understand," while patients who did not receive a post-visit phone call ranked in just the 40th percentile.

Closing the Gap

When Studer Group published *Excellence in the Emergency Department: How to Get Results* in 2009, we cited much evidence in the literature that demonstrated how crucial post-visit phone calls were to reducing preventable adverse events post-discharge. And yet, despite the fact that so many EDs are now making the calls, recent research still shows we have additional opportunity to close that critical information gap for our patients. In one 2012 study, only 43 percent of ED patients left the ED correctly informed about diagnosis, planned examinations, and follow-up.[31] Study authors noted that "standardization of discharge procedures and training physicians in how to ensure patients actually understand the information provided are needed."

While most organizations we coach tell us they are doing some form of post-visit call, it's frequently consistency of calls and lack of leadership that aren't maximizing the benefit of the calls. In a similar scenario, some organizations tell us they are calling 100 percent of patients, but perhaps reaching fewer than half.

To achieve the results we've described above in terms of clarifying discharge instructions, ensuring understanding of medications and side effects, and arranging for follow-up care, **best practice recommendation is attempting to call 100 percent of eligible patients with a contact rate of 60 percent or higher**. If you have a limited amount of time, call high-risk patients first. If you want to maximize your contact rate, call elderly patients on morning shifts and working folks on evening shifts.

Figure 4.5
Post-Visit Phone Calls - ED Satisfaction and Contact Rate

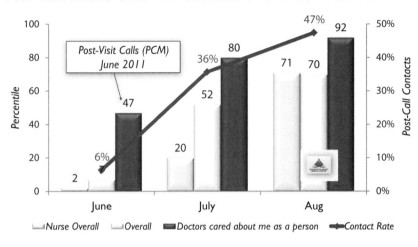

Source: Willamette Valley; ED Volume: 20,000

Note the positive correlation between the increase in ED patient satisfaction as this ED improved its contact rate with post-visit phone calls. Willamette Valley Medical Center in McMinnville, OR, began making post-visit phone calls in June 2011. In August, they attempted 97 percent of discharged patients and connected with 50 percent.

However, you may also want to choose a specific population to call if you suspect specific gaps. Typical populations include LWBS, patients who waited more than three hours, parents of very young children (under age two), or families of elderly patients (more than 75 years old). Or even perhaps a handpicked list of patients you believe may have experienced problems with their care.

In the ED at Kapi'olani Medical Center (affiliated with Hawaii Pacific Health System) in Honolulu, Alson S. Inaba, MD, division head of pediatric emergency medicine, has created a four-step policy to prioritize patients who receive post-visit ED phone calls.

A laminated card on computer terminals reminds physicians and nurses of the call priority.

In three years of making the calls and steadily increasing the percentage of attempts and contacts—the goal is to call 100 percent of discharged patients and reach 50 to 60 percent—Kapi'olani reduced 24-hour ED return visits by 13.3 percent in 2011 compared to 2008 before beginning post-visit phone calls. "Personally, I've been making post-visit phone calls to my ED patients in families for more than 20 years," says Dr. Inaba. "After all, my responsibility to them doesn't end when they walk out of the ED. It ends when they recover from their illness or injury. It's the right thing to do!"

Tips for Rolling Out Post-Visit Phone Calls

Who makes the calls? Ideally, the person who can make the most impact for the patient makes the call. That may be the person who cared for the patient, ED providers and nurses, or in the case of calls to patients at high risk for readmission, someone who can address those specialized issues on the call.

Review the concept of key words with those making the calls to assure the key words are aligned with those on the patient satisfaction survey that the hospital uses to measure ED performance. Also, ensure callers know how to apologize to ensure effective service recovery (e.g., "Thank you for that feedback. I am so sorry we did not meet your expectations. We are currently working on getting better in this area."). To review a sample template for making ED post-visit phone calls, visit www.FireStarterPublishing.com/AdvanceYourED.

Also, before rolling out post-visit phone calls, ask physicians to role model two to three calls daily to get buy-in from staff. Request that they share stories that show the impact on clinical outcomes of interventions resulting from the calls as well as wins and opportunities for improvement that they captured (e.g., "I called some of our patients today. Lori, Mr. Parker was very complimentary about your care. I also learned we have some real opportunity to be clearer with our discharge instructions.").

Remember, you may not change staff performance with patient satisfaction results or HCAHPS data, but you will change it by demonstrating how it verifies the quality of clinical care you are providing and saving lives! Be sure to consistently reward and recognize—both publicly and privately—those who are making calls.

Also, hold leaders and staff accountable for call goals by tracking post-visit call attempt and contact rates and reporting this monthly to leadership. At one organization, the CNO held a 30-minute huddle meeting every week where every nurse manager was required to give a two- to three-minute report on the effectiveness of their post-visit phone calls (e.g., about a clinical save, what they learned about care they provided, and a win they shared with a staff member). This level of accountability helps take performance to the next level.

A tip for leaders: Instead of asking staff, "How are those calls going?" be prescriptive. Say, "Tell me which processes you've been able to fix, who you've been able to recognize, and what you've learned about the care we provide." Review data regularly. What are your patients telling you? Are key items being identified for process improvement?

We find that an organization's ability to hardwire a process that feeds back what patients say on the calls to ancillary departments, ED staff, and others directly correlates with how well organizations are able to move results and sustain the gains using post-visit phone calls.

Five Tips for Effective Post-Visit Phone Calls: Taking It to the Next Level

1. **Identify potential adverse events during the call.** If you're discussing medication side effects, for example, ask the patient if he is experiencing any nausea, vomiting, or shortness of breath. Be specific with the question to ensure the patient can anticipate and respond quickly if needed.

2. **Use the physician's name early.** Begin the call by saying, "Hello, Mrs. Simpson, Dr. Iverson asked that I call and check on you." By using the physician's name right upfront, you alert the patient that this is a clinical call and also manage up the physician's care and concern for the patient's well-being.

3. **Focus your call on clinical outcomes to identify care gaps.** For example: "Were your discharge instructions clear and understandable?" "Are you having any unusual symptoms or problems?" "Have you filled your new prescriptions yet?" "Were you able to make a follow-up appointment?" By saying, "Tell me how you're caring for yourself at home," you can verify that what they say matches the discharge instructions.

4. **Capture feedback for the ED.** By asking if there are any physicians or nurses you can recognize for providing very good care—and then hardwiring a system to share that

in the ED—you verify you are providing the type of care you believe you are delivering.

5. **Close with a thank you.** By asking if the patient has any further questions, you capture actionable opportunities for process improvement.

Accelerating Post-Visit Phone Calls for Efficiency and Clinical Process Improvement

Following up on what patients tell us is *critical*, so accountability can't be optional if an organization wants to get and sustain results. Many find that Studer Group's Patient Call Manager^{SM} (PCM) software is the best solution for tracking.

To ultimately prevent readmissions, Studer Group recommends creating diagnosis-specific questions for high-risk patient populations (e.g., a heart failure patient could benefit from multiple calls to ensure continuing compliance and measuring tangible indicators to measure their recovery).

PCM also allows for documentation into the medical record. Additionally, it ensures accountability by measuring patient contact details by units and/or individual callers, to close gaps for greater staff compliance if patients are dropping off the call lists because they're not being contacted within 24-72 hours.

Even if you use a paper/pencil process versus automation, it's no longer an option to keep the logs in a big box in someone's office. There is often required clinical follow-up and documentation, so centralization and standardization ultimately help.

Many organizations are also using the "teach back" method for higher-risk groups. Instead of asking, "Do you have questions about your medications?" they may frame the question around "Tell me how you're administering your medications at home." This improves compliance and ultimately will prevent readmissions and extend the continuum of care—something that will be mandatory with future CMS regulations.

To learn more about effective post-visit phone calls, watch "Sending Them Home Prepared: Well-Executed Discharge Instructions and the Patient Experience," a Studer Group webinar at www. StuderGroup.com/Webinars.

So there you have it: If your organization is already using AIDET, Hourly Rounding in the ED and reception area, and/or post-visit phone calls, but just not moving results, you now have the tools and tactics to take them to the next level. Always connect back to the reasons why these tools raise the standard of quality patient care to motivate your staff; be prescriptive in the way you communicate with patients; and always ensure a continuous cycle of quality improvement by feeding back both the wins and opportunities for improvement that you capture with these communication tools.

Key Learning Points: Advanced Communication Tools

1. There are three advanced Must Have communication tools: AIDET, Hourly Rounding in the Emergency Department and ED reception area, and Post-Visit Phone Calls. All three improve clinical quality and respond directly to key drivers of patient priorities as measured on patient satisfaction and HCAHPS surveys.

2. AIDET (Acknowledge, Introduce, Duration, Explanation, and Thank You) is a highly effective evidence-based, prescriptive communication framework that improves ED patient perception of care, reduces anxiety, and creates a culture of *always* when used with every patient every time.

3. When the eight behaviors of Hourly Rounding in the Emergency Department and ED reception area are used prescriptively and consistently, this practice reduces LWBS patients, falls, and call lights, while improving patient satisfaction and giving nurses back more time.

4. Post-visit phone calls are the best four minutes in healthcare! They improve clinical outcomes, save lives, reduce readmissions, and connect providers and nurses back to purpose, worthwhile work, and making a difference. While staff may resist them initially, no one ever wants to stop once they start! The value becomes clear to clinicians.

CHAPTER 5

Skills Validation
and Verification

"Vision without execution is hallucination."
—*Thomas Edison*

Now that you're familiar with the advanced Must Have tools and tactics to move ED performance, how will you be sure they are executed correctly and consistently? That's where skills validation and verification techniques come in. They ensure these practices occur with every patient every time. Essentially, they are "gap finders" when we're seeking to hardwire new behaviors.

What do we mean by "hardwiring"? Hardwiring is defined as validation that the behavior is used 90 percent of the time with the prescribed frequency, utilizing prescriptive skills, and eliciting actionable reward and recognition and process improvements that are documented and followed up upon.

Nine Questions to Ask to Ensure Behaviors Are Hardwired

1. Was education provided to all who are expected to adopt the behavior?
2. Was the *why* over-communicated?
3. Did leaders make clear that the behavior was mandatory?
4. Were new behaviors practiced using role-play?
5. Is the new behavior measured, quality verified, and compliance audited?
6. Are results of verification reported transparently?
7. Are leaders giving positive feedback immediately when excellent performance is observed?
8. Are leaders consistently correcting poor performance immediately on the spot?
9. Are there consequences for continued non-compliance (up to and including termination)?

The four validation and verification techniques used to ensure tactics are hardwired include: (1) simulated skills labs, (2) direct observation, (3) leader rounding on patients, and (4) post-visit phone calls.

Simulated Skills Labs: Start with Training

The simulated skills lab model can be used to diagnose and close performance gaps in almost any prescribed behavior (e.g.,

Must Have). For the purposes of illustration, we'll take you through examples of how to validate AIDET with a skills lab, although they can be used to validate leader rounding, Hourly Rounding in the ED reception area and treatment areas, and so much more. (Studer Group coaches use competency checklists to validate all skills trained.)

It works like this: First, train leaders and staff. Then ask them to role-play what they've learned in a "safe" environment while coaching and giving feedback.

Typically, training consists of a 30-minute didactic presentation where you explain why the tactic is important, what the tactic is, how to do it, and connect back to purpose, worthwhile work, and making a difference by explaining how the tool addresses clinicians' goals to provide quality patient care. If you are a Studer Group partner, you can access video vignettes at www.StuderGroup.com/LearningLab to show what "right" looks like and assign trainees to watch them prior to your presentation.

In fact, many of these training resources are available at www.StuderGroup.com. Physicians, for example, can watch an excellent four-minute video by Studer Group's Wolfram Schynoll, MD, on enhancing communication skills with AIDET at www.StuderGroup.com/Insights/EnhancingCommunication. Nurses may want to read and view Regina Shupe's *Insight* on "The Power of Our Words" in preparation for AIDET training.

As always, over-communicate the *why* when training by connecting back to quality patient care. Also, share the evidence, data, and studies that demonstrate better outcomes when using the tactics. After you connect to clinical quality, you may want to share evidence from other organizations that have been successful with these practices.

If you're training physicians on AIDET, you might share some data like this:

Figure 5.1
UAB Improves Patient Perception of Doctor Care

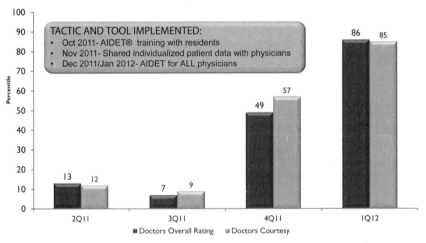

* University of Alabama Birmingham; discharge date

By validating the use of AIDET and making individual physician data transparent, the University of Alabama at Birmingham Hospital in Birmingham, AL, improved overall patient perception of doctor care from the 13th to the 86th percentile.

Next, break into small groups and role-play various scenarios. If you are training on AIDET, you could demonstrate how to use this communication tool effectively on a first patient encounter, how to use it with a patient in pain, one who is upset with wait time and in a hurry to leave, or any other scenario common to your ED.

Skills labs are teaching and coaching opportunities to accelerate performance of a skill you have already trained. Use them to identify gaps between what providers, nurses, and ancillary staff believe they are doing and what they are *actually* doing.

In coaching 100 nurses recently on Hourly Rounding, for example, we began by asking nurses if they were noticing a decrease in patient falls and if their call lights had decreased due to their Hourly Rounding, giving them more time to care for patients. "Absolutely not!" they immediately chorused. Clearly, there was a performance gap we needed to address.

You'll first want to determine the focus of the skills lab by diagnosing key opportunities for improvement. Consider once again PPD—the top priorities of ED patients—as well as the high correlation between patients' "likelihood to recommend this hospital to others" and how well the ED addressed top patient priorities.

Be sure to include this "voice of the patient" in your assessment. Also consider hospital priorities based on HCAHPS composites scores (e.g., MD/RN courtesy and respect, clarity of explanation, time spent with patient, explanation of medications and common side effects of medications, pain management).

AIDET, leader rounding on patients, and Hourly Rounding in the ED reception and treatment areas typically have a high impact on improving all of these metrics, as they did for the ED at Satilla Regional Medical Center in Waycross, GA.

Take a look:

Figure 5.2
Satilla ED Moves Performance

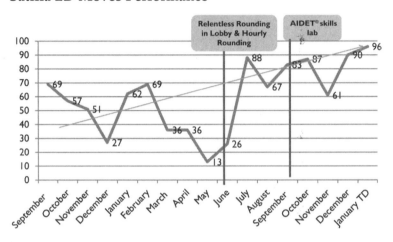

By hardwiring Hourly Rounding and using an AIDET skills lab to accelerate performance, Satilla's ED jumped from the 69th to the 99th percentile in a large national patient satisfaction database with respect to "informed about delays" over a one-year period.

Setting Up for Skills Labs

Who should participate in a skills lab? Key stakeholders who interact with ED patients, including ED physicians, physician assistants, nurse practitioners, RN/LPNs, ED techs, secretaries, security, and transporters. In one organization, for example, we put security guards through skills labs because they frequently had patient contact when locking up valuables while patients were getting tests and treatment. AIDET skills labs evaluated how well they acknowledged and introduced themselves, explained what they would do with the valuables, how long it would take to get them back, and ensured a thank you at the end of the patient interaction.

You'll also need to recruit some leaders as actors to serve as the patient in the bed and a family member, as well as coaches and evaluators. Choose these from among the ED leadership team. You might choose the ED medical director, ED assistant medical director, ED director, manager, assistant nurse manager, educator, or a charge nurse.

If you're training many individuals, consider setting up several rooms for the skills lab, each staffed with actors (to simulate patients) and at least one coach so that you can conduct the lab with small groups of three or four people. This way, trainees feel less intimidated than they might otherwise feel with a one-on-one evaluation. Plus, you'll be providing extra learning opportunities as individuals who wait their turn hear the feedback you give others.

Let's use AIDET once again as we walk through an example of a skills lab. During the lab, you'll ask each of the trainees to use the prescribed behavior they've learned in the scenario you present. So for a physician participating in an AIDET skills lab, for example, you'd expect to see her greet the patient and wash her hands thoroughly first. Did she shake the patient's hand? Sit down? Was she very prescriptive as she walked the patient through AIDET? Did she close with a sincere thank you? Each individual should take about 20 minutes to run through the lab.

Finding Performance Gaps

Sometimes, the performance gaps become immediately clear. At one organization we coached recently, the chief nursing officer played the patient in the bed. The first time a nurse came into the room and demonstrated AIDET, she had an "Aha!" moment. She realized they had been using AIDET for 16 months without moving communication results because while staff were introducing themselves, they were not managing up their experience, setting an accurate expectation for duration, or closing the loop with the patient by letting them know when they would return.

At another organization, patients routinely rated lab personnel poorly. When we put an inexperienced lab technician through an AIDET skills lab, we noted that instead of knocking and waiting to be invited in, she loudly yelled, "Lab!" and walked right in. When asked why she was doing this, she responded that that was what she'd been taught to do. She was more than happy to offer a more prescriptive response when coached. Almost immediately, the patient's perception with lab services jumped from the 5th to 90th percentile!

At the completion of the role-play, the facilitator will begin by offering positive feedback on what was done well and ask other leaders (actors) in the room to share their positive feedback as well. Then he may hone in on one or two key opportunities for improvement and ask the individual to focus on those over the next 90 days. Overall, the skills lab should be a positive experience for the trainee, with many compliments and one or two clear areas for improvement.

Over the past year, Studer Group has trained thousands of ED physicians, nurses, and support services staff on the importance of the AIDET communication framework. Here are trends we've noted:

Top Things Providers and Nurses Should *Start* Doing	Top Things Providers and Nurses Should *Stop* Doing
Sit down/shake hands when entering the room to evaluate the patient.	No longer use vague words and statements (e.g., "hopefully," "as soon as possible").
Manage up self, staff, and hospital team.	Stop using hard-to-understand medical terms with patients. (Instead, ask patients to repeat back next steps to ensure they understand.)
Address duration—give more specific time frames (e.g., "in the next 45 minutes" versus "as soon as possible").	Reduce use of non-specific, non-measurable terms such as "in a little while," "pretty soon," or "right away."
Offer a more memorable introduction to reduce anxiety. (e.g., "I am Dr. Pratt and I will be the emergency physician in charge of your care today.")	Failing to introduce self or not sharing relevant experience. (This builds trust and confidence with the patient.)

In conducting skills labs across the country, we have found that almost all learners demonstrate basic AIDET skills. However, **one of the biggest opportunities for nurses is to be more prescriptive when managing pain and also utilizing our own nursing care plans.**

For example, if I am the nurse treating a patient with an ankle injury, I may say, "Here are three things I can do to manage your ankle pain before the doctor comes in. I'll elevate it, apply an ice pack, and position it more comfortably." An additional opportunity for nurses includes a better explanation of medications and addressing potential medication side effects. For all healthcare providers, nurses and ancillary services, there is opportunity to maximize the use of key words regarding safety, privacy, and comfort.

Whether you're using skills labs for AIDET—as in the example above—or using them to validate other Must Haves like Hourly Rounding in the ED reception area or leader rounding, you'll note trends in opportunities for improvement with your population of learners.

Set Post-Training Expectations

Be sure to set expectations with those who have just completed skills labs so they understand that you will be using direct observation and leader rounding over the next 90 days to validate smooth and consistent execution of the skills you just evaluated. Explain that you will be conducting additional skills labs in 90 days to further validate and accelerate skills based on what you are observing. If you are rigorously using this cycle of maximizing skills in simulation labs and then consistently validating skills through direct observation and leader rounding, you should hardwire the trained behavior for impressive results within six months.

Once staff and leaders are trained, leaders should observe and validate in a live environment over the next 90 days. You can directly observe clinicians' interaction with patients, and also as leaders, by rounding on patients.

Taking Leader Rounding to the Next Level

While SG considers leader rounding as a foundational Must Have, we'd like to revisit best practices briefly here because it's such a critical verification and validation tool. Watch an actual video of a leader rounding on patients in the ED at www.Studer-Group.com/LearningLab. This link is available to Studer Group coaching partners only.

One of the reasons leader rounding is so valuable is because of the real-time feedback you get from patients on how well you've hardwired the behaviors you are working on. Leader rounding gives you an opportunity to know right *now* how well your staff are communicating and assess the care that is being provided in your Emergency Department.

The best practice recommendation for leader rounding on patients in the ED is to consistently round on 25 percent of treat-and-release patients within a 24-hour period. For example, in an ED with an average daily census of 100 patients per day that admits 20 of those patients, the goal is to round on 20 of the 80 treat-and-release patients. (Always round on 100 percent of patients holding for an inpatient bed!)

Who rounds? The nurse manager, ED medical director, or the charge nurse. Remember, your goals when leader rounding on patients are to manage the patient's expectations, ensure service recovery, harvest recognition/manage up providers and staff, and gather key information for coaching staff to the next performance level.

Be prescriptive in your communications with patients. When managing expectations, say, "Our goal here at Baptist Hospital is to provide you very good care. Have we met your expectations today?" If the patient responds, "Well, everything is okay now, but I had to wait a long time in the waiting room," you have a real-time opportunity for service recovery.

You could reply, "I'm really sorry about that. We don't like anyone to have to wait when they come in for emergency care. We know that sometimes this occurs and we appreciate your patience. I am so sorry you had to wait." (The good news: As AIDET becomes hardwired in your organization, there will be much less need for service recovery!)

When rounding, ask yourself the following two key questions: (1) "What have I learned about the care being provided to this patient?" and (2) "What must I do with this information?" You could, of course, do nothing...or yell and scream if things aren't going well...or even fix it for the patient. But those behaviors won't help you meet your mission of providing consistently high-quality patient-centered care.

In fact, sometimes we hear leaders complain that they don't have time to round on 25 percent of ED patients. Frequently, it's because they are spending their time providing too much nursing care during leader rounds rather than validating the care they expect to see being delivered and providing service recovery if necessary! Remember, this is a short visit. It shouldn't feel rushed to patients. Typically, many leaders round in three to five minutes per patient. (If you do find the patient has additional care needs, share them with the primary nurse, rather than providing the care yourself. This creates accountability for the direct caregiver and helps reduce time needed for the rounds.)

Unless it's necessary to intervene for patient safety, your goal is to collect information on the leader rounding log to understand how well staff are using the behaviors you trained them on. To download a copy of the leader rounding log, go to www.FireStarterPublishing.com/AdvanceYourED. This creates a continuous feedback loop from patients/families back to staff with wins and opportunities for improvement.

So in the case of AIDET, for example, when you ask, "Do you know what your plan of care is?" and the patient responds, "Yes, I'm going to have an x-ray," you've just validated Explanation. If you ask, "Do you know when that's going to occur?" and the patient tells you the nurse said "as soon as possible" rather than "in the next 15 minutes," you've identified an opportunity for that nurse to be more prescriptive about Duration. If you ask, "Who's done a great job for you?" and the patient can't think of a single name, you've identified an opportunity to enhance the Introduction.

Once you have completed daily rounds, it's important to give immediate positive feedback and also share opportunities for improvement with the caregivers of those patients.

A sample conversation might sound like this: "Hi, Jessica. I just wanted to give you a little feedback. I rounded on three of your patients today and they all said such positive things about your care. They were very appreciative and wanted me to know how well you've communicated with them. One thing I did notice was that only one of your three patients had a call light in their bed so I want to make sure you understand the expectation of our department is that every patient—no matter how ambulatory and alert that patient is—must have a call light in their bed."

If you have a nurse who is under-performing, collect good data before approaching them with opportunities for improvement. You might, for example, round on 10 of their patients to collect objective evidence that prescriptive behaviors have not been used consistently with their patients. Providing this aggregate data to the nurse demonstrates a trend for needed improvement instead of a one time, anecdotal situation.

Coaching conversations should always be professional and positive, sharing at least one win (there's one in every encounter...even if it's just that the bed linens are clean!), then objectively describing opportunities for improvement, and reaffirming our expectations. To hear another sample conversation based on leader rounding in the ED, log on to www.StuderGroup.com/LearningLab/Leader-RoundingED to watch a short video vignette. This link is available for Studer Group coaching partners only.

Figure 5.3
Leader Rounding Log for Validation

ED Validation Rounds									

Name of rounder _____ Date_____ Shift_____ Rounded With:_____

Patient Name Room #	Who is caring for you today? (AIDET)	What are we doing for you today? (AIDET & PPD)	Do you know what you are waiting for and how long? (AIDET & PPD)	For patients c/o pain - What have we done to manage your pain? (PPD)	Do we check on you frequently and update you about your care?	Call light in reach?	White-board updated?	Leader Interventions:

NOTES:

Download a full-size template at www.FireStarterPublishing.com/AdvanceYourED.

Use Tiering to Prioritize Leader Rounding

We find that best practice EDs maximize the impact of their leader rounds by tiering and then prioritizing their rounds based on skills lab scores. This can be a particularly effective way to quickly maximize the impact of AIDET for physicians, for example. All physicians are ranked from one to five based on their demonstrated competency. Next, they are sorted into Tier 1, 2, and 3 categories for priority leader rounding based on the volume of patients they see. A physician who has a low AIDET competency score and sees a high volume of patients would be a high priority (Tier 1), whereas a physician who has a high AIDET competency score and sees a low volume of patients would be a lower rounding priority (Tier 3).

Validating with Post-Visit Phone Calls

As we discussed in Chapter 4, we make post-visit phone calls for a number of reasons: to ensure patients understand post-visit instructions, confirm they understand their medications and potential side effects, reduce readmissions, and identify opportunities to reward and recognize our staff.

In addition, as with leader rounding, post-visit phone calls offer us the same type of real-time opportunity to validate the quality care we believe we delivered. Once a post-visit call is completed, we can take immediate action based on this real-time feedback from our patients regarding their perception of care. We don't have to wait five to six weeks to read it in comments on a survey!

In summary, to ensure that agreed upon tactics are executed consistently, we highly recommend using simulated skills labs to validate competency and identify skill gaps. We are then able to continue coaching our staff to the next level of performance by ensuring leaders are rounding on patients. Once we have executed a post-visit phone call, we've closed the loop. In other words, we have a complete picture, as a leader, of the care we are providing.

Just remember, as former President Ronald Reagan once stated, "We must trust but verify!"

Key Learning Points: Skills Validation and Verification

1. While many providers and staff are using AIDET and other Must Haves at hospitals nationwide, they don't always get the results they are seeking due to undiagnosed performance gaps. The best ways to validate and ensure any of these skills are hardwired is through the use of skills labs, direct observation, leader rounding on patients, and post-visit phone calls.

2. After new skills are trained on, providers and staff are validated through skills labs (20-minute role-playing scenarios with hospital personnel serving as actors) in small groups. A coach completes a competency checklist and offers positive feedback and opportunities for improvement to each individual.

3. Through direct observation and leader rounding on patients, leaders can track staff performance on new skills that were validated in the skills lab for real-time feedback, wins, and coaching opportunities. Using a rigorous cycle of skills labs and leader rounding, organizations can hardwire new behaviors for impressive results within six months.

4. In addition to their many clinical benefits, post-visit phone calls offer us another way to obtain real-time actionable feedback to validate the quality of patient care we expect that we have delivered.

CHAPTER 6

Coaching for Performance

"The key is not the will to win. Everybody has that! It is the will to prepare to win that is important."
—*Bobby Knight, winner of 902 NCAA Division I men's college basketball games*

If your ED staff are like many, you may hear them say they can't do leader rounding or post-visit phone calls because they don't have enough time; they don't feel it's necessary; or it just isn't comfortable. The good news: You can successfully address all of their concerns! We see leaders do it every day.

The #1 Barrier to Change: Addressing Staff Resistance

In the many years Studer Group has offered its two-day Excellence in the Emergency Department Institute for ED leaders, physicians, and nurses, we've surveyed thousands of attendees prior to the conference to ask what they perceived to be the top barrier to change. The number one answer is *always* staff resistance!

If you're experiencing this problem, first ensure that you've set good goals and metrics to track them, that you've clearly defined expectations, and that you've adequately trained and coached staff as we've outlined in earlier chapters. Next, check your sequencing of tools and tactics. Have you overwhelmed the team by asking them to implement five new behaviors all at once? If so, you're risking that "change fatigue" we mentioned. Focus on those one or two priority goals to fix flow bottlenecks first!

Sometimes staff just don't think it's that important to do things exactly the way you've requested. They don't understand how what you're asking them to do connects to quality patient care. In those cases, connect back to the *why*. You can say, "Tell me what's not right about this for the *patient*? While it might be uncomfortable for us, we need to find ways around the barriers if it delivers better patient care." Once we know a better way to do things, our values dictate that we must do so.

Another problem is that staff might feel offended that you are asking them to do a behavior in a way other than what they prefer. When they just aren't compelled by the evidence-based data for best practices, you may need to get tough and ask: "Why is your personal agenda more important than the team's agenda?"

Since the goal is to reduce variance and maximize results, you'll need to get comfortable asking staff to be more prescriptive when necessary. If you don't, you will enable a culture of optionality, leaving a portion of the results on the table due to individual variance.

Fears, Myths, and Misinformation

It's also possible that staff are reluctant due to lack of "skill" (they still don't understand how to correctly execute a behavior) or "will" (they just have lots of excuses for why they can't do it).

When it comes to "will," the truth is that their concerns are often grounded in fears, myths, and misinformation. Let's review some of the most common things we hear:

"Our scores are low because patients are unreasonable."

The reality is that if you compare thousands of Emergency Departments in large databases of performance by patient satisfaction survey vendors, the data doesn't bear this out. The real reason your ED is being outperformed is because other EDs are improving their performance more quickly than your ED and excelling in "top box" performance.

The greatest difference between EDs that are in the top quartile in percentile ranking versus the bottom is the percentage of patients who score the ED as "very good" rather than "good." (Actually, unreasonable patients are a very small percentage of the total number of patients!)

"Our patients don't fit the model."

Every ED feels they have a unique patient population... whether it's a high percentage of elderly patients, poor patients, mean patients, ED super users, or homeless patients. (Guess what? Those homeless patients are not returning your surveys!) And in fact, it turns out that meeting basic human needs with care, compassion, and communication is universally appreciated, whether your ED is located in the US, UK, Canada, or Australia.

"If we do all this, we'll attract the wrong patients!"

The perception is that if we create a best-in-class ED, all of the most undesirable patients (e.g., super users, those who can't pay for their care) will flock to our ED. But actually, we find the exact opposite to be true. A top ED attracts patients who value quality care. In fact, the payer mix typically becomes more favorable as word of mouth spreads about the excellent care experience.

"I didn't go into medicine to kiss their butts!"

While we all went into emergency medicine to save lives, resuscitate, and intubate, the reality is that the vast majority of patients we see do not have life-threatening illnesses. They are reasonable patients with wide-ranging acuity. This isn't about "smile school" or "scripting"; it's about using evidence-based tools for effective communication to ensure quality clinical care for all.

"Perception doesn't really matter."

Actually, it matters more than ever. It directly impacts quality clinical outcomes. The fact is, consumer expectations have changed drastically over the past 40 to 50 years. They changed first from a "paternalistic" view where patients did what doctors told them without question to a more "consumeristic" view where patients felt entitled to quality care, sometimes based on Internet misinformation. Then watchdog groups emerged. And now finally, we've moved to a more "mutualistic" model where patients seek to partner with their providers, be included in treatment decisions, be kept informed, cared about as a person, and shown dignity and respect. They frequently want assistance in filtering the glut of health information.

"The hospital is just trying to make money."

The reality is that hospitals are just trying to stay solvent in the face of healthcare reforms that require more transparency, reporting, and reimbursement based on their performance on quality clinical outcomes and patient perception of care.

With value-based purchasing about to go into effect in the U.S. as this book goes to press, many hospitals are at risk for huge cutbacks in reimbursement if they don't meet baseline thresholds for Medicare reimbursement based on "Always" performance on eight HCAHPS composites and 12 clinical process core measures.

An example: Imagine a 276-bed hospital with a 22-bed ED. It has a 45 percent Medicare payer mix and $630 million in patient revenue. A 1 percent reduction (based on base DRG operating payment adjustments of 1 percent for 2013) will put more than $2.8 million at risk. If we fail to improve ED performance—which impacts inpatient performance—we will be forced to respond to increasing volumes with fewer resources.

Set Clear and Transparent Goals and Objectives

In Chapter 2, we shared the process for aligning goals, cascading them effectively, and tracking performance with a daily dashboard. Many organizations use a "thermometer" approach much like United Way uses to measure successful fundraising efforts. These can be included on communication boards within the ED that share key information under the Five Pillars: People, Service, Quality, Finance, and Growth. (To see sample communication boards, log on to www.FireStarterPublishing.com/StraightA.)

Here's an example of one "thermometer" approach for patient satisfaction:

Figure 6.1

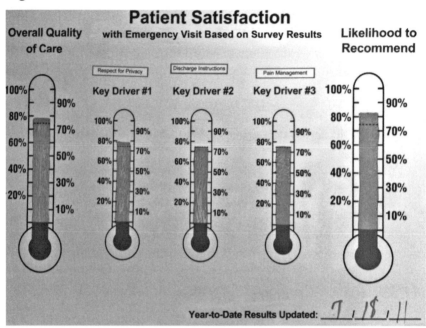

The key is to be transparent with staff on how the ED is performing to goal. Don't share a complicated Excel spreadsheet with lots of data. Rather, use an at-a-glance format that is simple and clear. We can begin to coach staff and providers to higher performance only if they first understand our goals and how well we are currently performing.

Use Objective Metrics to Drive Accountability and Ongoing Surveillance

In Chapter 5, we shared how leader rounding is a critical validation and verification tactic for evaluating staff performance because we can harvest reward and recognition to identify performance gaps for prescriptive feedback. For example, if you have a nurse with low patient satisfaction, you may learn when rounding that 8 out of 10 of his patients don't have an up-to-date communication whiteboard, don't know their plan of care, or don't feel their pain is well managed. You have just captured some extremely objective data for a low performer conversation, as we'll discuss below.

When it comes to improving physician performance, sharing actual objective data with physicians is critical. Because physicians want to perform at a high level and they also respond well to comparative data, Studer Group recommends using a "patient perception of care scorecard." Here's one example:

Figure 6.2
Sample Physician Scorecard for Patient Perception of Care Metric

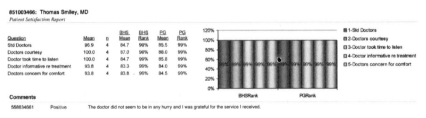

The physician scorecard measures an individual physician's performance on objective measures of patient perception of care (based on patient survey results), including standard doctor care, courtesy, and "took time to listen." This data measures this physician's performance against the survey vendor's entire physician database and includes actual comments from this physician's patients.

In the same way, physicians should receive a scorecard rating them on clinical quality. Many EDs use a Five Pillar scorecard so physicians can see how they are trending on key goals under People, Service, Quality, Finance, and Growth. In the example below, individual performance metrics are tagged green (for trending at or above goal), yellow (slightly under goal), and red (far below goal):

Figure 6.3
Sample ED Physician Scorecard

Pillar	ED Score Card	Dr. John	Smith			
	Metric	Peer Avg.	Goal	Jan 11	Feb 11	Mar 11
	ASA/beta-blocker for AMI	92%	95%	98%	90%	94%
Quality	Blood cultures on CAP	90%	95%	91%	93%	100%
	Antibiotics within 4 hrs for CAP	88%	95%	93%	90%	95%
	EKG for syncope patients over 50	94%	98%	99%	92%	94%
Service	Patient Satisfaction (percentile)	60%	75%	64	66	62
	Complaints (avg per month)	0.2	0.1	0	0.1	0.2
People	Door-to-doc times	42 mins	30 mins	50	46	44
	Peer Review (1-5)	4.3	4.5	N/A	N/A	4.6
	Nurse Review (1-5)	4.1	4.5	N/A	N/A	4.2
Growth	Likelihood of recommending	68%	75%	78	74	69
	Left without being seen rate	3.8%	2%	3.9	3.6	3.5
Finance	Patients per hour	2.2	2.5	2.1	2.2	2.0
	Avg patient charge	$229	$229	$280	$265	$222

Meeting or exceeding goal
Above peer avg., below goal
At or below peer average

This physician is doing well in meeting clinical quality goals, but has clear opportunities for improvement in metrics that measure service and finance.

Also, transparent data is more compelling than veiled data for driving physician performance. Likewise, physicians are more sensitive to comparative data rather than individual raw data. Remember, physicians want to be successful. No physician wants to be ranked below his or her peers. And yet, physicians don't always correctly perceive their own performance until they view objective metrics that tell the true story.

By graphing the scores of each physician compared to his or her peers, physicians can see how they stack up, like in this example:

Figure 6.4
Physician-Specific Performance 2012

However, it's important to gauge whether your organization has the maturity to begin this process with complete transparency. Some organizations choose to blind the names initially when sharing comparative data as above, so that only the actual physician being coached can see how he compares to his colleagues. Over time, such organizations frequently move to a model of complete transparency. (As we suggested, you have to get comfortable being uncomfortable to effect real change!)

Coaching Staff and Physicians

Studer Group recommends using highmiddlelow® performer conversations to rerecruit top performers, develop middle performers, and create accountability using an "up or out" approach with low performers. Unfortunately, in many EDs, leaders spend 80 percent of their time on the 5 percent of employees who are not meeting expectations. Your goal should be to spend more of your time with the employees you want to retain: the other 95 percent!

While low performers can be tenacious, the real solution to moving performance of the ED team is to engage and rerecruit high and middle performers. This creates an increasingly uncomfortable gap as low performers become further isolated from better-performing employees. As a result, low performers improve or leave, unlocking the full potential of the team for peak performance.

Highmiddlelow conversations are one-on-one coaching conversations with employees. Since high performers are those you most trust, these conversations focus on "rerecruiting" them by rewarding and recognizing their efforts. Tell them where the organization is headed; thank them for their work very specifically; tell them why they are so important; and ask if there is anything you can do for them.

Middle performers are typically the largest group of employees in the ED. They're solid performers you would rehire who have opportunities for development. They may lack the confidence, skills, or experience to work at higher levels, or perhaps they're newer employees.

Use a Support-Coach-Support model to reassure, rerecruit, and develop them. Begin by assuring them you want to retain them and expressing how valuable they are by providing specific feedback on what they are doing well (Support). Then offer one specific opportunity for improvement and the benefit of growing in this area (Coach). Conclude by reaffirming your confidence in their ability to develop and expressing gratitude for their current contributions (Support).

Use the DESK Model with Low Performers

As you might guess, low performer conversations are the most difficult conversations. This will not be the first time the low performer has heard about performance issues, so your goal is to express clear performance expectations and specific consequences for not achieving goals in a designated timeframe.

Begin by avoiding small talk and instead objectively **D**escribe their current performance, behavior, and/or attitude gaps. Then **E**valuate their performance and share your disappointment with it; **S**how the employee specifically what is expected of him; and **K**now (share) the consequences of not improving performance. Follow-through is key to success. (For more information on highmiddlelow, visit www.StuderGroup.com. You can access many articles as well as video vignettes on what real high, middle, and low performer conversations look like.)

Tips for Coaching Physicians

Because physicians can be difficult to replace, it's important to invest in their success, particularly middle performers who may just need some coaching to improve dramatically. Otherwise, the organization faces steep financial, emotional, and clinical costs when they leave.

While it might be appropriate to email a blinded version of the histogram in Figure 6.4 to all physicians before your highmiddlelow conversations, you will want to discuss the data individually in a confidential one-on-one meeting.

Frequently when coaching, we find that some physicians overestimate their performance. Experiment with this by blinding the physician names on the X-axis and asking the physician where she thinks she is. Sometimes physicians will become emotional when they learn how much lower they are actually performing than their colleagues. Other times, the reverse is true. They underestimate their performance and are elated to learn they are performing higher than anticipated.

You can quickly get a sense of how coachable and committed a physician is to moving his results by how well he takes ownership of his data. If a physician is in the lowest percentile, but had no idea and is very receptive to coaching, you can anticipate large gains in performance with remediation and tactical training.

Some physicians need time to go through the five stages of grief—denial, anger, bargaining, depression, and acceptance. Others absolutely will not take ownership of the data and instead will play the "we/they" game (i.e., "The reason patients complain about me is really because the nursing staff aren't friendly and this place moves at a snail's pace.") This may be a sign of an "uncoachable" physician.

Physicians learn best from physicians they respect. So choose a physician champion—someone who is visionary, well regarded by her peers, high-performing, clinically astute, and who role models the intended skill sets and behaviors—to officially lead this process. This individual will need to create trust in the measurement tool and not accept excuses from low performers. **However, even a qualified physician champion will succeed only with consistent, solid support from senior leaders**.

When this book's coauthor Dan Smith, MD, was appointed physician champion in 2007 to lead the ED patient satisfaction journey at Baptist Health System/Emergency Physicians Affiliates (EPA) in San Antonio, TX, he faced 45 semi-enthused physicians, but developed a system of transparency, accountability, and learning while introducing and tracking physician performance on patient satisfaction.

In trying to set up physician coaching meetings, there was an occasion where one physician was not responsive and always had reasons why he didn't have time to meet. Because the CEO of the emergency medicine group was aligned, he sent an email to the physician that read: "Dr. X, as you are aware, our patient perception of care is very important to the success of our organization. I need you to meet with Dr. Smith within the next week for your coaching session. If you are uncomfortable with this, please email me and I will meet with you."

Coincidentally, the physician responded the very next day with his availability. With aligned messaging and efforts, EPA increased the percentage of physicians in the top quartile of performers from 20 to 50 percent of the group in a mere six months. Overall patient satisfaction with ED physicians of this group increased from the 20th percentile rank in 2007 to the 80th percentile rank in 2011 in a large national patient satisfaction database. EPA has sustained a trend line of improvement for the last five years by using this coaching method.

When coaching a low-performing physician, be objective with your comments using the DESK model. For example,

Describe: "Dr. Myers, you've had six complaints from patients related to behavior and attitude issues, and this is reflected in similar negative comments on patient satisfaction surveys over the past six months. Nurses comment that you refuse their requests to go back and inform the patients and answer their questions. As a result, these patients leave the ED upset and frustrated. The nurses do not feel supported when this happens."

Evaluate: "Joe, these behaviors are contrary to our group credo and the very communication model that we all have diligently worked to hardwire. No one wins in these situations, and you set yourself up for risk. I'm extremely concerned when I hear about these negative behaviors."

Show: "I need you to change your approach when interacting with patients. Use AIDET, sit down, listen to them, and show some empathy. They aren't looking for hours of time—just a few minutes and some dignity and respect. I can tell you that this construct works, and not only will you eliminate these complaints, you will be viewed as a team player and your patient ratings will improve dramatically."

Know: "We are going to closely monitor this matter. If I hear or read of similar negative interactions over the next quarter, this matter will be elevated by Administration to the Medical Executive

Committee. That's the hospital's policy. Your renewal contract with our group would be placed in jeopardy. Do we have clarity about this? We will meet again in 90 days."

TeamHealth Coaches Physicians to Higher Performance

"I find that most ED physicians who are low performers simply aren't aware that they are low performers. Once we share their individual performance with them and they see how they rank against their colleagues, many are very motivated to change," explains Robert Strauss, MD, FACEP, senior vice-president and chief medical officer of TeamHealth East and chair of TeamHealth's LDI committee. TeamHealth contracts physician management and staffing services with more than 450 Emergency Departments nationwide. "Utilizing AIDET, key words, and coaching high, middle, and low performers is improving both the satisfaction with and the performance of our practitioners."

At one TeamHealth ED—with an ambitious goal of moving from the 30th to the 90th percentile in overall physician satisfaction in one year—it turned out that the lowest ranking physician was the medical director. While he is a great physician, patients perceived him as rushed since he rarely maintained eye contact and frequently stood at the door during patient interactions. By coaching him through AIDET and cuing him on a few key behaviors, including sitting, making eye contact, using "key words," and closing questions, his performance quickly jumped to the 95th percentile.

At another ED, a physician who perceived himself to be a strong patient advocate was devastated to learn his performance ranked behind all his colleagues. "He knew he was a bit cynical," explains Strauss, "but he didn't realize his patients were perceiving him as negative. With coaching and feedback, he jumped from the 21st to the 98th percentile in overall physician satisfaction, which he has maintained."

Remember, don't skirt the issue when having difficult conversations with low-performing physicians and staff! If patients are rating a physician poorly due to behavior or attitude issues (like yelling at the patients or refusing to talk to them), he needs to know. Ask him to sit down closely to the patient, lower his voice, and listen. Then review his patient satisfaction data again in 90 days. Once he sees a performance improvement after changing his bedside approach, he will be very likely to embrace these new behaviors. If he does improve or shows glimpses of positive change, reinforce the "win" and encourage more of the same efforts. Share some hope and positive reinforcement. It goes a long way toward keeping physicians engaged.

Hold Monthly Supervisory Meetings

The purpose of a monthly meeting between supervisors and leaders is to confirm the effective use of accountability tools to achieve results. By reviewing progress to goals on the individual's annual evaluation, we can course correct if work priorities aren't well aligned.

Leaders should bring these items to the meeting: their leader evaluation and goals, monthly report card, any industry/external environment issues, 90-day work plan, follow-up assignments from the organization's Leadership Development Institute (i.e., LDI linkage grid), rounding logs, thank-you notes, and any issues around people trends (e.g., peer interviewing, results from the leader's 30/90-day meetings with employees) or standards of behavior.

For these meetings to be effective, they must occur monthly. Also, leaders need to communicate expectations to direct reports in advance of the meeting, focus on positive outcomes first, and confirm and document action items to complete before the next meeting.

There are four key components to the meeting: first, reviewing the leader's performance (via a monthly report scored by the supervisor to summarize results to-date). Then verifying key behaviors that are being used to achieve results (e.g., Rounding for Outcomes). Next, leaders and supervisors review the LDI linkage grid to confirm the status of completing those assignments. The final component is a brief discussion of professional development (e.g., which skills they need to enhance to accelerate performance and what resources are available to assist them). Many senior leaders choose to begin the supervisory meeting by rounding on their direct report and conclude the meeting by covering any miscellaneous items that are noted in the "parking lot" part of the agenda.

Figure 6.5
Sample Monthly Meeting Agenda

	Monthly Meeting Agenda (Date of meeting)	Leader: (Name of Senior Leader)
Pillars-Organizational Goals	**Agenda/Minutes** FYI – for your information FD – for discussion FA – for action or decision	**Action Items**
Tip: *Trust, then verify*	▪ Do not accept *"We're working on it"* ▪ Ask to see evidence or hear outcomes/timelines	
Leader Evaluation	▪ **Monthly Report Card Results and 90-Day Plans-** (leader to bring updated score card to meeting)-(FD) ❑ Current Results ❑ Review 90-day action plan for all goals not at target ❑ Are tactics specific and measurable? ❑ How is leader communicating and holding staff accountable for 90-day Plan action items? ❑ How is leader coaching Must Haves® behaviors to support 90-day Plan? i.e. Rounding for Outcomes, AIDET/Key Words, Peer interviewing, 30/90-day questions	
Rounding For Outcomes	• **Outcomes from Rounding- Employee, Patient and Internal Customer Rounds-** (FD) ask a sampling of questions to assess the effectiveness of rounding ❑ Rounding Wins ❑ Who have you recognized this week? Who should I recognize? (Thank-you notes) ❑ What issues are you currently fixing? What have you fixed this month? What trends are you seeing? ❑ What people trends are you observing? Who is being coached to a higher level of performance? ❑ What tough questions are you hearing? ❑ How are you communicating rounding wins/trends back with staff? ❑ How are you utilizing the pillars and Standard of the Month to support outcomes?	
Linkage Grid	▪ **Linkage Grid** from LDI (FD) review actual linkage grid from last LDI, ask more drill down questions, such as: ❑ Percentage of staff trained on AIDET? Competency achieved? How have you recognized staff who are consistently demonstrating AIDET®? ❑ Standards of Behavior? Wins? Tough situations? Counseling anyone for noncompliance?	
Hardwiring of Must Haves®	▪ **Compliance with:** ❑ Rounding on employees, patients, and internal customers ❑ Thank-You Notes ❑ Employee Selection- Peer interviewing, 30/90-day questions ❑ AIDET/Key Words ❑ Pre- and Post-Visit Phone Calls ❑ Leader Evaluation Goals ❑ Communication Boards	
Parking Lot		

Download a full-size version of this sample agenda at www.FireStarterPublishing.com/AdvanceYourED.

In our journey to create a best-in-class Emergency Department, understanding the *why* of our journey is the most important driver of behavioral change for both staff and physicians. By becoming aware of common barriers to change and also fluent in openly addressing these concerns and questions, you'll pave a path for change. But at the heart of effective coaching for performance is transparency and one-on-one coaching with staff and physicians. By developing a shared understanding of baseline levels of "service/quality fitness" and clarity around how to close individual performance gaps to meet organizational goals, you've just set the stage for maximizing your impact as a team…for consistent collaboration in the ED, the hospital, and ultimately your community.

Key Learning Points: Coaching for Performance

1. Staff resistance is the number one barrier to change. However, you, like thousands of other ED leaders, can successfully dispel fears, myths, and misinformation by explaining the real *why* to achieve breakthrough performance in your ED.

2. Set clear and transparent goals and objectives. Many EDs use United Way-like "thermometer" goal boards for visibility and transparency in sharing how the ED is trending to goal. Avoid communicating with complex spreadsheets that require prolonged analysis to decipher performance.

3. Use objective metrics to drive accountability and ongoing surveillance. Leader rounding is a very effective way to evaluate staff performance. For physicians, use scorecards that measure individual performance and provide comparative data with peers.

4. Use highmiddlelow performer conversations in one-on-one sessions to drive individual performance. Studer Group's DESK (Describe-Evaluate-Show-Know) model is a very effective "up or out" approach for low performers.

5. When coaching physicians, you will quickly get a sense of a physician's commitment to improving performance by how well he takes ownership of his data. Don't skirt the issues. And remember, senior leader support and alignment are key!

Collaborate
Consistently

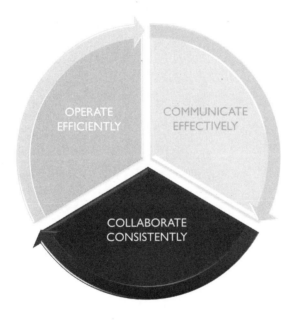

CHAPTER 7

Driving Collaboration within the ED

"Perfection is not attainable, but if we chase perfection,
we can catch excellence."
—*Vince Lombardi*

In Sections 1 and 2, we shared how to align our goals and behaviors. Here, in Section 3, we'll focus on aligning our processes with those who support us in the ED. Consistent collaboration is the "secret sauce" that pulls the whole model together and differentiates a truly great ED from a good one.

While you can download sample communication tools at Studer Group's website or develop your dashboard for improved operations based on best practice metrics we offered earlier, consistent collaboration is something that is built over time...it requires a demonstrated commitment to creating and sustaining a true culture of teamwork.

Because emergency medicine is so complex and unpredictable, it's impossible to achieve and sustain performance goals without active collaboration among providers, staff, and senior leaders. Consistent collaboration also ensures more timely care for patients and aligns with those top ED priorities (PPD).

This ensures we deliver better quality outcomes and improve patient perception of care, because we demonstrate more courtesy, respect, and communication. In fact, in one 2010 survey of more than 220,000 Australian consumers,[32] patients said one of their greatest desires was for nurses and doctors to work well together. Collaborative and cohesive teamwork also means lower turnover and less absenteeism, which translate into better employee retention for higher quality patient care.

Figure 7.1

Low Employee Turnover = Lower Patient Mortality

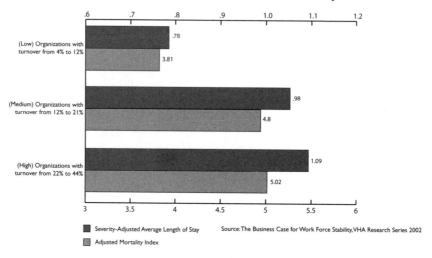

The results from this study show how organizations with low employee turnover experience lower rates of patient mortality. As turnover increases, so does patient mortality.

Studies also show that highly engaged employees also perform fewer workarounds, improving the organization's ability to hardwire a culture of safety.

Figure 7.2
Employee Engagement and Safety Link

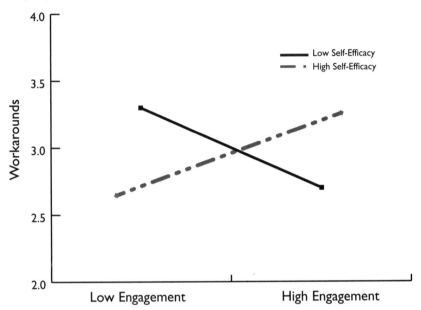

Source: Leadership, Rework and Workarounds; Grant T. Savage, Ph.D.; University of Alabama at Birmingham, February 2011

It's not surprising that when you talk with providers and staff, their basis for a "good day" is usually more about how the team performed and the collaborative environment, rather than technical achievements. To build this kind of culture, make a point of consistently rewarding and recognizing behaviors you want to reinforce. Comment frequently on what's going well, rather than on what's going wrong.

Studies[33] show that to achieve a *positive* relationship with someone, the ratio of compliments to complaints is three to one. A two-to-one ratio will achieve a *neutral* relationship, and a one-to-one ratio creates a *negative* relationship.

The Art and Science of "Managing Up"

At Studer Group, we define "managing up" as positioning a team member in a positive light to other team members and patients. Imagine an exhausted ED technician who is finishing up his fifth shift in a row. He may view himself as a "minor" contributor to the team.

Now imagine a physician saying this to a patient about his tired employee: "Hang in there, Mr. Carter. Our ED nurse Josh here is one of our finest RNs and he is going to place your IV and get those tubes of blood to our lab and blood bank so we can get you that blood transfusion right away."

What do you think will happen next? Josh will rise to the occasion, place that line quickly, and dash off to the blood bank. And his follow-up to the physician will be something like, "Dr. Diaz, is there anything else I can do to help that patient?"

If you're wondering if managing up colleagues really means that much to them, we can assure you that it does. It not only energizes them, but it raises their commitment, improves their attitude, and reconnects them to a sense of purpose, worthwhile work, and making a difference. In fact, it leads to real collaboration and eliminates the "we/they" mentality (where one person makes themselves look better at the expense of another) that can block real culture change.

Because communication about the care provided is built into the managing up process, the person doing the managing up feels reassured that what is supposed to get done will get done. He's reminded during the handoff of how competent and capable that team member is. He's also viewed as a valued team member by the rest of the group.

Patients, of course, are the ultimate beneficiaries of managing up. Imagine a sick, anxious patient who needs all the reassurance you can offer. When she experiences a pair of providers who share the same agenda for her care and voice their high standards of care, she feels less anxious, perceives her care as more timely and compassionate, and will experience a better clinical outcome.

Don't view managing up as another task to do. Think of it as an adjunct to the communication framework we refer to as AIDET. In fact, a common place to manage up is during the "Introduce" phase of AIDET (e.g., "I see you've met Judy. She's a phenomenal nurse whose patients rave about her care and skill. She will place your IV within the next 15 minutes.")

Feel free, however, to manage up someone at any phase of AIDET. For example, when a newly bedded patient is waiting on a busy physician (Duration), the nurse can say, "Mr. Mitchell, Dr. Anthony will be with you in about 10 more minutes. Patients just love her because she is so thorough in her exams. She's with another patient now, but I know that she'll be giving you her full attention as soon as she arrives. Thank you for waiting."

If you've never managed up anyone, it will feel awkward at first. But as you experience the productivity and respect that results from using it, you'll be inspired to use it more frequently and make it part of your daily communication.

Taking Stakeholder Meetings to the Next Level

The ED isn't an island. Interdependency means you'll all need to work closely together to get results. To achieve and sustain real collaboration, you'll need to hardwire processes that allow for consistent input and engagement from ED providers, staff, ancillary and support departments, and the executive team.

High-performing EDs use a monthly stakeholder meeting to create shared ownership and ensure that the goals of the ED are aligned. Studer Group recommends using a formal agenda. (Download a sample Agenda by Pillar at www.FireStarterPublishing.com/AdvanceYourED). This 60- to 90-minute meeting typically includes the ED medical director, assistant medical director, nursing director/manager, permanent charge nurses, a few key staff physicians, and key ancillary and support leaders from Registration, Radiology, Environmental Services, and Security. As the team matures, meetings should last no longer than 60 minutes.

Ask your CEO, CNO, and vice president of support services to attend at least quarterly to support the group on issues like flow, throughput, team building, role delineating, and service. This will help drive results and accountability. However, everyone doesn't need to attend every meeting. Invite stakeholders as needed who have an impact on your current agenda items.

For example, if the ED is working on improving the efficiency of front-end flow to decrease turnaround times, the stakeholder meeting can provide an opportunity to talk through the perceptions and suggestions of registration staff. You'll need to work closely and collaboratively with them to ensure you are minimizing the time the patient enters the ED until the time they are taken to the back and treated. You'll also need to ensure you are maximizing your quick registration and bedside registration processes so you can pull them to the back as soon as a bed is open. You'll need to ensure you have a process in place to maximize collection of copays up-front. These are all goals shared by the ED and registration.

Typically, at stakeholder meetings, you'll identify barriers to improvement as either people or process issues. In one ED we visited recently, as we walked through some of these above processes at a stakeholder meeting, we learned that 10 percent of patients were leaving without a complete registration. As ED physicians became more efficient at treating low-acuity patients quickly, the registration staff was missing opportunities to register patients before the physician discharged them.

This communication gap was having a huge negative financial impact on the hospital because it couldn't collect on patients who weren't registered. At the stakeholder meeting, the group agreed to implement a quick registration process before patients were seen by providers and nurses. Caregivers agreed to notify registration staff before discharging patients so they could complete a full registration.

At another organization, the ED was focused on preventing 72-hour returns with timely post-visit phone calls, but found they frequently had wrong phone numbers on file and couldn't reach patients who had been discharged in 72 hours. By working with registration staff at stakeholder meetings, registration staff agreed to use new key words by telling patients, "We may call you post-discharge to check on you and ensure you're doing well. To ensure we have the proper phone number in our system, can you confirm your number, please?"

(A side note: Studer Group's Patient Call Manager software tracks the percentage of wrong phone numbers. We frequently find that EDs have greater than 10 percent of wrong numbers for patients! If this is true for your ED, you are going to have difficulty impacting your 72-hour return rate with post-visit phone calls, due to suboptimal contact rates, until you address this issue.)

If you're working on aligning goals and processes for middle flow issues, you'll want to ensure that the staff who can impact those metrics—Radiology, Lab, Respiratory Therapy—attend. If you're focused on back-end issues, include the hospitalist, in-house supervisors, and in-house nurse managers to maximize collaboration for moving patients out of the ED.

Tips for Effective Stakeholder Meetings

1. Use a formal agenda for this monthly meeting.
2. Share objective data results. No anecdotes!
3. Be sure to invite the stakeholders who impact key agenda items.
4. Recognize that performance barriers are always people or processes. (Address low performers using highmiddlelow. Improve processes through stakeholder collaboration.)

Round on Internal Customers

Just as leader rounding on patients is the number one way to obtain immediate information for coaching your staff, leader rounding by ancillary and support departments (e.g., Radiology, Lab, Security, Registration) on ED leaders is the number one way to ensure these stakeholders are aligning their behaviors for efficiency to improve ED flow and provide quality patient care to meet our mission.

When ancillary and support service department leaders round, they open clear lines of communication and remove barriers, so that caregivers are not being taken away from patient care to focus on non-patient activities. Just as nurses are evaluated by patients and families with patient satisfaction surveys, ancillary and support services departments are evaluated by an internally developed interdepartmental survey. Each of these survey tools complements the rounding process by identifying focus areas for resolving challenges and implementing best practices. Progress can then be validated during rounds. By rounding proactively between monthly stakeholder meetings, leaders can course correct as needed.

When leaders of ancillary and support departments round in the ED, Studer Group recommends they use key words such as "Our goal is to provide excellent service to your department. I will be rounding on you every month and wanted to spend about 30 minutes with you today."

Also, use key words to provide examples of improvements that have resulted from rounding. A food service leader might say, "Last month we discussed the opportunity to improve food items for the Emergency Department. Over the course of the last month, we have started stocking frozen meals for off shifts to utilize. Since then, how have they been utilized by the staff for patients? Has this helped with providing hot meals during off shifts?"

What Right Looks Like: Sample Key Words

- "What is my department doing well?"
- "Is there anyone specific I can recognize for doing great work? What have they done?"
- "What one or two things can my department do better? Any ideas on how we can improve?"
- "Our department wants to respond in a timely manner so we are focusing on our responsiveness. Can you share a time when you had to wait for a response from our department? What are you typically waiting to receive?"
- "I will be back next month to round again. If there is anything we can do before that time, please get in touch with me."

Develop a rounding plan. When ancillary and support department leaders are rounding on key customers (like the ED), plan to round a minimum of one hour per week, which should allow a leader to round on two departments. Leaders who should be rounding in the ED include those from Environmental Services, Materials, Pharmacy, Imaging, Lab, Food, Respiratory Care, and others as needed. All ancillary and support service areas should be rounding on departments they serve. These will be departments that have a high impact on strategic goals (e.g., high-volume, high-risk, priority goals based on interdepartmental survey results).

Also, be sure to schedule an appointment or identify the best time of day for rounding. If you're a leader of an ancillary department rounding on a nurse manager, for example, make an appointment or ask what the most convenient time of day is for her. Most importantly, use a rounding log to capture feedback for actionable data based on what internal customers tell you.

Figure 7.3
Sample Log for Leader Rounding on Internal Customers

LRIC5: ROUNDING LOG

Date: _____   Unit rounded on: _____   Manager Name: _____

Last Month Rating on Support Service Evaluation: Current Rating on Support Service Evaluation:

_____   _____

AREAS OF FOCUS:

STEPS	KEY WORDS AND GUIDE	COMMENT / NOTES
AIDET®: Acknowledge, Introduce, Duration, Explanation and Thank you	A: Acknowledge, eye contact and say hello…. I: "My name is <xxx> and I have worked in <dept> for <x> yrs…" D: "I will be rounding on you <state frequency> and wanted to spend about 30 minutes with you today…" E: "Our goal is to provide excellent service to you and will discuss specifically how to best help you serve our patients…" T: "Thank you for your time today…"	
Establish Rounding Expectations	Ex: "Can you tell me three things that mean excellence to you and your staff?"	
Accomplishments: Review what has been accomplished	Ex: "Since I rounded with you last, I want to highlight the following items/systems put into place based on feedback…"	
Collect Wins: What is my department doing well?	Ex: "What is our department doing well?"	
Harvest Recognition: Who from my dept has impressed you lately? Why?	Ex: "Is there anyone specific I can recognize for doing great work? What have they done?"	
Opportunities: What can my department do better? Any ideas on how we can improve?	Ex: "What is one thing you would like us to address right now?" OR "What one or two things can my department do better? Any ideas on how we can improve?" (provide timeline)	
Focus areas: • If an inter-department survey is in place, identify specific areas from the survey process to address. • If your department is not surveyed, you can still assess key customer expectations.	Ex: "Our department wants to respond in a timely manner and we are focusing to improve our timeliness." "Help us learn…can you explain a time when you had to wait for a response from our department?" "Now tell me, when we do not respond in a timely manner, what do you typically wait to receive…?"	
Teamwork: Is there anything I can help you with?	Ex: "Are there any other questions you have or anything else I can help with right now?"	
Follow-up: Establish next rounding date and document the round	Ex: "I will be back <date> to talk again. If there is anything we can do before that time…"	
Appreciation and Thanks	Ex: "Thank you for your time…"	

To download a full-size log for leader rounding on internal customers, visit www.FireStarterPublishing.com/AdvanceYourED.

Once ancillary and support departments have harvested ideas and concerns through rounding, they can use a stoplight report to keep their ED customers current on progress towards resolving outstanding issues. By posting a stoplight report on communication boards, staff can easily see which items have been addressed, which items are in progress, and which items cannot be completed and why.

Figure 7.4
Sample Stoplight Report

Department/Unit	Supported by:	Date:

GREEN/COMPLETE	YELLOW/WORK IN PROGRESS	RED/CAN'T COMPLETE AT THIS TIME AND HERE'S WHY

To download a full-sized stoplight report template, visit www.FireStarter-Publishing.com/AdvanceYourED.

Use a Hospital Support Card

Many hospitals use a formalized process—a hospital support card accessible via the organization's Intranet—to request monthly feedback from clinical leaders on support from ancillary/support departments. On a monthly basis, clinical leaders are asked to rate these departments on a scale of 1 to 5 on accountability, timeliness, accuracy, attitude, and operations. Results are averaged and reported on a support card like the one below. This is yet another important tool for ensuring the ED has the support it needs to meet goals and get results.

Figure 7.5
Sample Support Card

							Department
						Main Support Card Page /Logout	X 3 East
							X 3 Usen
June 12, 2010							3 West
							4 South, Pain Management
*BB-Brad Balon x6584 | PP-Paul Ponte x6407 | WS-Bill Sullivan x6549 | KO-Kevin O'Connor x6533 | SC-Steven Clark x6015 | SM-Scott MacLean x6043							4 Tanger West
							X 4 Usen
							6 East
Department - Director/Manager*	Accessibility	Timeliness	Accuracy	Attitude	Operations	Average	6 Usen
							6 West Peds
Biomed - BB	4.67	4.60	4.67	4.67	4.67	4.65	Adult GI
							X Central Supply
Engineering - WS	4.70	4.20	4.56	4.80	4.63	4.58	Emergency Dept
							Henderson Day Surgery (DSU)
EVS - PP	4.64	4.64	4.70	4.64	4.70	4.66	X ICU
							X Lab - Administration
Equipment - PP	4.75	4.60	4.25	4.75	4.67	4.60	Lab - Blood Bank
							Lab - CE & Pathology
Food Service - KO	4.75	4.75	4.75	4.75	4.75	4.75	Lab - Chemistry
							Lab - Cytology
Linen - PP	4.86	4.71	4.86	4.88	4.86	4.83	Lab - Hematology
							Lab - Histology
Pharmacy - SC	4.80	4.80	5.00	4.80	4.80	4.84	Lab - Microbiology
							Lab - Phlebotomy
Supplies - BB	4.50	4.56	4.56	4.56	4.56	4.54	X Maternal Child Health
							MGH Radiation Oncology
Transport - PP	4.80	4.50	4.60	4.80	4.60	4.66	X OR Control Desk
							X OR Pod 1
Information Svs - SM	4.57	4.43	4.57	4.57	4.57	4.54	X OR Pod 2
Average	4.70	4.58	4.65	4.72	4.68	4.67	X OR Pod 3
							PACU
							Pre-Op
Rating Department	Service	Rating	Shift	Note			Pre-Testing
							Radiology - CT
Lab - Administration	Engineering - Attitude	5	1	Always a great attitude.			Radiology - Interventional
							X Radiology - Main X-Ray
Lab -	Engineering -	3	1	TAT			Radiology - Mammography
							Radiology - MRI
							Radiology - Nuclear Medicine

In this hospital, the lowest scoring departments are Engineering, Supplies, and Information Services. By sharing transparent data, these support departments can identify their performance gaps and develop a plan to improve performance for a score above 4.75.

Pre-Shift Huddles Align Staff and Move Results

Now that you've aligned interdepartmental goals at the monthly stakeholder meeting and ancillary and support departments are rounding on clinical leaders in the ED to provide strong and consistent support, it's time to share that feedback—and other real-time information on progress towards goals—with individual ED staff and physicians at daily huddles.

A "huddle" is a quick five- to ten-minute meeting at the beginning of a shift change where the charge nurse or clinical leader uses a standardized agenda (See Figure 7.5) to inform and motivate staff, as well as remind them about expected behaviors that are being hardwired. It's a key tactic to use to keep staff informed about departmental goals and performance expectations to achieve desired outcomes.

The purpose of the pre-shift huddle is to drive care to the highest quality and provide the safest care by keeping all team members on the same page and working toward the same goals. To learn more about how often to huddle, how to use reminder cards in huddles, and other effective tips on huddles, see Chapter 9 in *Excellence in the Emergency Department: How to Get Results*.

If reducing LWBS patients is a key goal in your ED, you might say at the huddle, "Great job yesterday. We saw 120 patients and only two patients left without being seen. Remember that our goal is that no one leaves. If someone is going to leave, please contact the charge nurse to intervene." Or likewise, if you are working on flow: "We've agreed to an expedited triage process. That should be five minutes or less, and yesterday it was 15 minutes. Why do we think we were off track yesterday? Moving forward today, my expectation is to keep triage to five minutes or less. The charge nurse will help monitor this."

As discussed in Chapter 2 on aligning goals and metrics, be sure to focus on making—and acknowledging—progress on priority goals as measured by the dashboard at daily huddles. If you are working on immediate bedding, remind staff at the huddle that the patient needs to be placed immediately in a bed 24/7, when beds are available. If you're rounding hourly in the ED reception area, share the results of your review of the rounding logs. You might say, "The good news is that we're doing it about 75 percent of the time, but we're not doing it consistently in those crucial late afternoon hours when the ED is so busy."

Essentially, you are sharing the hard data with them and reinforcing expected behaviors with every patient every time to ensure you meet those goals.

These are all examples of how to use the daily dashboard at pre-shift huddles to drive goals that roll up to the monthly dashboard and ultimately to leader evaluation goals (www.Studer-Group.com/LearningLab/EDPreShift). This link is available to Studer Group coaching partners only.

Use a Standardized Huddle Agenda

Here's a sample standard agenda for pre-shift huddles:

Figure 7.6
Sample Standard Agenda for Pre-shift Huddles

1. WINS / CONNECT TO PURPOSE LETTER / STORY	
2. ED UPDATE – PROCESS CHANGES	
3. DAILY DASHBOARD REVIEW	
Daily volume	
# of patients who left without being seen	
Number of patients admitted	
ED LOS Goals:	
• Length of stay for discharged patients	
• Fast Track turnaround time - times:	
• Disposition to Discharge to IP Unit	
4. PATIENT PERCEPTION OF CARE TRENDS	
Hourly Rounding®	
Post-Visit Calls	
Leader Rounding on Patients	
5. STAFF RECOGNITION	
Introduction of New Staff	
Birthdays	
Recognition from Rounding on Patients	
6. OTHER	
(Include other brief information that the staff needs to give great care and have a great day)	

Download a full-size blank standardized agenda at www.FireStarterPublishing.com/AdvanceYourED.

Begin pre-shift huddles by sharing the wins (e.g., a connect-to-purpose story, patient thank-you letter, performance of yesterday's team). This is a great place to share reward and recognition that leaders have captured during their rounds on patients. Then review daily dashboard results so everyone understands how close the team is to meeting its goals and what it needs to do to continue to close the gap. (See Chapter 2 for examples of a daily dashboard.)

The huddle is also an excellent opportunity for providers to share a "medical minute" with staff. Perhaps physicians or mid-level providers share information about new medications or medication side effects they're seeing, or how the entire team impacts the departmental flow of patients. Providers appreciate the opportunity to serve as leaders and educators, while staff appreciate the opportunity to learn.

Next, review the tactics the team is working to hardwire (e.g., Hourly Rounding, post-visit phone calls) and share both wins and opportunities for improvement. And finally, close with any other brief information staff need to give very good care and have a great day.

St. John's Hospital Captures Early Wins with Huddles

Thirty days ago we started pre-shift huddles and are already finding this five- to ten-minute stand-up meeting is very well attended by RNs, EDTs, HUCs, and providers. It creates a shorter pause in shift change—a 10- to 15-minute improvement—since everyone quickly receives all the information they need for a good shift.

The huddle has also helped us get key information—like assuring patients have call lights for safety and real-time positive results of the first few weeks of our immediate bedding project—out to a wider audience for better buy-in, focus, and partnership. This creates even more momentum for results. We're also seeing some wins with collaboration between our medical and nursing teams. Physicians seem to appreciate the charge nurse's invitation to join these nurse "stand-up meetings."

Staff tell us they like the just-in-time updates about things like drug shortages, the opportunity to ask clarifying questions, and also hearing when things are going well...like how the outgoing shift rallied on a high-volume day recently when they couldn't even get a lunch break.

As leaders, we love the opportunity to quickly and publicly recognize individuals who go above and beyond every shift—such as the housekeeper who received several compliments recently—and the team, for their high participation in our annual employee engagement survey—so we can all celebrate the wins together.

Overall, we're finding that the huddles provide a forum for our dedicated and engaged leaders to explain the *why* behind our requests, listen to staff concerns and questions, and create a collaborative environment for a true transformation in our ED.

—Peter Tanghe, MD, ED medical director, and Tamara Ducklow, RN, BHS, BCEN, ED clinical director
St. John's Hospital, HealthEast Care System, Maplewood, MN

Essential Components of Pre-Shift Huddles:

- Led by charge nurse/supervisor/manager.
- Include physicians and mid-level providers.
- Utilize standardized agenda.
- Keep it short. (No more than five to ten minutes!)

Tips for Success:

- Formalize training/expectations for charge nurses with respect to pre-shift huddles and a review of the daily dashboard.
- Include a section in the charge nurse binder for daily huddle notes to drive consistency in huddles throughout the day.
- Directly observe pre-shift huddles.
- Ensure updated and accurate results of the daily dashboard.
- Round on staff to inquire about the effectiveness of the pre-shift huddle.

If you are a Studer Group partner, please visit the Studer Group Learning Lab at www.StuderGroup.com/LearningLab/EDPreShift to watch a 10-minute video of what an actual effective pre-shift huddle looks like.

The Importance of Peer Interviewing
and Consistent Onboarding

No discussion of how to create and sustain collaboration in the ED would be complete without touching on the importance of consistent onboarding of new employees. By ensuring we select the right people, we protect the culture we've worked so hard to create.

Best-in-class EDs begin prescreening prospective employees by asking them to sign an attestation that says they agree to adhere to the organization's standards of behavior. Standards of behavior can address any key behaviors at work, ranging from good manners (knocking before you enter a room or office) to positive attitude markers (smiling or saying "thank you"). Be clear with applicants: Say, "If you don't feel you can sign the attestation and abide by the standards, the selection process should end right now."

Prior to the interview, use the job description to define core competencies a candidate would need to possess to be a high performer. Work with your team to gather their input on essential skills and characteristics to look for in the interview.

Then conduct peer interviews. If you've ever made a poor hiring decision, you know it's a mistake with lasting consequences. Chances are good that your staff figured out that the new hire wasn't going to work out well before you did. Studer Group finds that while leaders typically prescreen for the organization's values and ask questions based on needed key competencies and experience, they frequently fail to recognize that job success is also about "fitting" in with coworkers.

Peer interviewing engages your high performers in the selection process. After you, as the leader, are satisfied the candidate is worthy of hiring, ask a panel of peers to conduct a group interview. (Staff members feel free to ask frank questions because the leader is not included in this interview.) Choose peer interviewers who are high performing and would work closely with the potential employee if hired.

Set them up for success by training them on how to use behavioral-based interview questions. To get the most from a behavioral interview, you'll need to train interviewers to listen carefully to the candidate's response. Use active listening, giving full attention to the other person. It's important to concentrate on what is being said while putting aside one's own need to reply or ask a question.

Lend an EAR to the Candidate

Use the "EAR" model to record the individual's answer after you ask a core competency question in a peer interview.

"**E**" refers to the event (or story) with which the candidate responded.
"**A**" refers to the action the person took.
"**R**" was the result or outcome of the experience.

When taking notes, use this EAR model to capture key details the candidate shares.

Because past behavior is the best predictor of future performance, interviewers will want to concentrate on questions that ask how candidates would *act*, rather than how they would *feel* or *think*. That's why peer interviews are organized around behavioral-based questions. These questions are geared to the competencies you've identified and are open-ended, requiring an example or story as the answer versus a simple "yes" or "no."

Behavioral-based questions are typically organized around skills and accomplishments, stability, goals, work environment preferences, communication skills, customer service, teamwork, supervisory and leadership skills, problem-solving, coping skills, prioritizing, creativity, initiative, diligence, personality/temperament, integrity/trustworthiness, and a few closing questions (e.g., "Why should we hire you?" "Do you have any questions for us?"). To download a copy of sample behavioral-based questions in each of these areas, visit www.FireStarterPublishing.com/AdvanceYourED.

Teamwork and problem-solving skills are two areas that are critical to success in the ED so hit those areas hard with questions like:

- "What behaviors do you find irritating in others? How do you address this?"
- "Describe a situation when you worked with a person whose personality was the opposite of yours. How did you deal with it?"
- "Tell me about a situation where you blew it. How did you resolve or correct it?"
- "Tell me about an experience where you turned a problem into success."
- "What were the major obstacles you overcame at your last job?"

When you use behavioral-based questions like these, you will see straight into a person's soul! Ask the panel to decide ahead of time who will "own" certain behavioral-based questions during the peer interview. Also, provide interviewers with a peer decision matrix to evaluate each candidate and rank that person based on responses received. The interview matrix is completed following each interview, before interviewing the next candidate so that candidates are analyzed independently. (Avoid assigning ratings during the interview.) Each interviewer completes their own matrix.

Figure 7.7
Sample Peer Interview Decision Matrix

Core Competency Area (Behavior Question/s)	Wt 1-3	Score	Total	Comments
Competency: Critical Thinking	3	3	9	
Competency: Planning and Organization	3	3	9	

To download a full-size sample of a peer interview decision matrix template, visit www.FireStarterPublishing.com/AdvanceYourED.

If anyone on the interview panel recommends the candidate not be hired, the candidate is not hired. Remember, if you as the leader have already pre-screened the candidate to go forward for peer interviewing, you will be happy with any candidate they choose. (Not honoring the recommendation of the panel is disrespectful of the team and will undermine the process.) A final tip on peer interviewing: A thorough behavioral-based interview takes 60 to 90 minutes.

Tying It All Together

Once you've hardwired your monthly stakeholder meeting, are rounding on internal customers, and are using a hospital support card to track results, you've created an important feedback loop with key stakeholders who support the ED. By implementing pre-shift huddles with providers and staff, you've given them the real-time information and motivation they need to have a great shift and work together efficiently. By hiring right with peer interviews and behavioral-based questions, you'll build momentum for collaboration by ensuring the right "fit." Then you're ready for the next step: driving collaboration in the hospital.

Key Learning Points: Driving Collaboration within the ED

1. Consistent collaboration in the ED is the "secret sauce" that differentiates a truly great ED from a merely good one. It ensures more timely patient care, delivers better clinical outcomes, improves patient perception of care, and improves employee retention.

2. Monthly stakeholder meetings create shared ownership of ED goals by convening ED clinical, ancillary, and support department leaders to identify barriers and shared solutions to drive performance. Use a formal agenda and invite those who can impact goals in current focus areas.

3. Rounding on internal customers is the number one way to ensure ED stakeholders are aligning their behaviors to improve flow and meet our mission of providing quality care. Use a rounding log to capture actionable feedback. A stoplight report keeps everyone current on progress toward resolving issues identified during rounding.

4. Just as nurses and physicians are rated on patient satisfaction surveys, clinical leaders can share feedback with ancillary and support leaders by rating them on an internal monthly survey. A hospital support card reports average departmental scores to prioritize action items.

5. Peer interviewing and behavioral-based interview questions create consistent onboarding of new employees and ensure a right "fit." Use the EAR model to practice active listening in interviews. Then rank candidates using a peer interview decision matrix.

CHAPTER 8

Driving Collaboration within the Hospital

"Culture outperforms strategy every time, and culture with strategy is unbeatable!"
— *Quint Studer*

At Studer Group, we find Emergency Departments that have hardwired the tools and tactics we've discussed so far are usually feeling pretty inspired and empowered by their results at this point. Typically, senior leaders, physicians, and others in the hospital have taken notice that the ED is gaining momentum and partnership with its monthly stakeholder meetings and daily huddles. They're impressed that the ED team has taken ownership of everything it can to fix challenges under its own "roof."

This is a great time to hardwire house-wide bed flow meetings twice a day if you haven't already done so. It's the logical next step. Typically, ED and inpatient leaders attend. Sometimes leaders from Radiology, Environmental Services, and Lab (e.g., "essential services") also attend.

Bed flow meetings are just a quick stand-up huddle to touch base. Is our hospital at capacity? What percentage of beds are filled? How many patients are coming out of PACU to be placed in beds? How many are being admitted through the ED? How many vented ICU patients are held in the ED?

(Of note: Objective standards that quantify overcrowding now exist. The National Emergency Department Overcrowding Score (NEDOCS), for example, calculates flow metrics for objective decision making on house-wide flow and NEDOCS-based surge plans. Visit www.nedocs.org.)

By collaborating on real-time patient flow, we speed inpatient admissions. Best practice—particularly for afternoon bed flow meetings—is to meet in the Emergency Department. Ensure the 3 p.m. house supervisor attends to share what the house status is and that ED leaders attend as a voice for the ED. (They should be familiar with the metrics from the daily dashboard they reviewed at the most recent shift huddle.)

By now, hospital leaders have probably also noticed that the ED has developed a very collaborative culture. And when they review the ED dashboard metrics, it may be clear that the barriers to realizing further efficiencies in flow are due to delays in transitioning patients from the ED to inpatient units.

What better time to enlist senior leader support for resources to finally address back-end flow issues? In this chapter, we'll share some best practices to drive collaboration within the hospital to reduce boarding, free up beds in the ED more quickly, and ensure a safe and efficient transfer for patients from the ED to inpatient beds.

Handoffs are a vulnerable time in terms of the potential impact on clinical quality, patient safety, and patient perception of care. In one example of a physician shift change handoff within an ED we coached, a physician just starting his shift was advised by the physician leaving to discharge a patient who presented with a bad headache if his CT scan was negative. However, a nurse approached him and said she felt uncomfortable discharging the patient as he had not improved after treatment.

Because that nurse spoke up and the physician was receptive to her inquiry, the oncoming physician reexamined the patient, communicated his findings with the patient and spouse, and recommended a spinal tap to "complete" the work-up. Ultimately, this revealed that the patient had meningitis. After appropriate treatment, the patient did well and had an uneventful recovery. This is just one of many examples of clinical saves—a culture that impacts quality and safety—that result from collaboration. (While the first physician received a complaint letter and the second physician received a thank-you note, who was the real hero? The nurse!)

The patient's experience in the ED will make or break the patient's overall experience in the hospital. The quality of that hand-off from the ED to the hospitalist is also critical as we'll discuss in a bit below.

Strategies for Engaging Physicians

To engage physicians and promote collaboration, it's critical to answer the question "What's in it for me?" Build a compelling case for collaborating with the team by sharing evidence on how a high-performing ED drives better clinical outcomes and patient perception of care. For physicians, the first considerations will always be: Is it right for my patient? Is it good for clinical quality? So always address the *why*—and the evidence for the best practice—before the *how* when asking physicians to change their behaviors.

As "captain of the ship," physicians set the tone for collaboration, both in the ED and across the hospital. Explain to physicians that when they role model collaborative behaviors, they become "contagious." For example, a physician can say, "Yeah, Joe, what do you have?" or she can say, "How can I help here?" See the difference? When staff watch a provider walk the talk about collaboration by providing a patient an explanation about the treatment she is ordering, they will do it too.

When physicians role model how to manage up using AIDET, for example, as we shared in Chapter 7, staff catch on quickly and emulate that behavior. This helps to break down silos and accelerates team performance. Physicians—like everyone else who works in the hospital—prefer to work with the "A team" because the quality of patient care is better and it makes for a great shift. Connect the dots for them. Show them how their ability to role model collaborative behaviors leads to higher retention with less absenteeism and turnover for better care. (See Figure 7.1 "Retention = Quality" in Chapter 7.) In the end, physicians can help create the very environment we all hope to practice and work in.

Another key to engaging physicians is to include them early in strategic planning and the rollout of new tools and tactics to drive performance. Ask for their input and opinions, rather than asking them to "sign off" on something the day before it's implemented. When you don't engage physicians early in the process, you are likely to end up with variable ownership and engagement, with physicians saying, "I wasn't part of strategic planning," or, "I sure wish I had been asked about this a year ago…"

Again, use the stakeholder model we shared in Chapter 7. Invite physicians to participate if they are key stakeholders in a particular process improvement. If your hospital is rolling out electronic health records and physician order entry, solicit physician input and feedback early!

Sometimes EDs can have the reverse challenge: when physicians move forward without engaging the rest of the ED. When diagnosing challenges in an ED in the southwest, for example, we found that because the physician champion was so focused on improving the performance of the ED physicians and provider group through AIDET and performance measurement, he had neglected to collaborate with nurses on the implementation of these tools. As a result, the performance of the ED physician group improved, but overall performance of the ED remained static, so the overall patient experience did not change.

This ED would've seen an earlier and more dramatic impact on performance by aligning the emergency physician efforts with those of ED nursing. Lesson learned: When embarking on a new strategy, whether it be a communication tactic or flow process change, align and cascade the strategy to all stakeholders (physicians and staff) who would benefit from it for the biggest impact on patients and their care.

Collaborating with Hospitalists: Best Practices for Patient Safety

What makes this handoff so important? First, as we noted earlier, more than 50 percent of hospital admissions come through the ED, and increasingly, hospitalists are on the receiving end of these admissions. Second, we know that effectiveness of early and timely care in the ED can improve not only quality outcomes (early resuscitation and optimization of therapy, for example, in cases of sepsis) but also patient perception of care. When we set a positive tone of care and communication from the outset, we impact the patient's entire hospital experience as mentioned above.

To drive effective collaboration between the ED and the hospitalist, it's key to understand the needs of both physicians as well as patients. This guides best practices in handoffs, preserves collaboration and trust, and improves outcomes in quality and perception of care.

What does the ED physician need? He wants a hospitalist who is receptive, a quick, smooth handoff, timely provision of inpatient orders, and timely movement of the patient from the ED to an inpatient bed.

Here's an example of a hospitalist's response to an ideal report from the ED physician:

"Very good, Dr. Roth...the patient has rapid AFib with mild CHF and is doing well on a Cardizem drip and cannula oxygen. She is a known DNR, which you confirmed with the daughter. Sounds like she is stable for PCU. Dr. Francisco, her cardiologist, is on Telemetry now, so I'll let him know she is here. Go ahead and get me the patient's ED nurse and I will give orders. Thanks so much!"

Here's what a hospitalist needs:

- A succinct yet complete patient report.
- The name of the primary care physician.
- A clear explanation of relevant "hot button" issues (e.g., code status or end-of-life care, family requests, or nuances in their clinical care or work-up).
- Early contact with requested consultants.
- "Manage-up" of the hospitalist by the ED physician.
- No "overstatements" to patients about specific inpatient tests/procedures.
- Time-sensitive, sound medical care for the underlying problem.

Here's an example of what a great report from an ED physician sounds like from the hospitalist perspective:

"Hey, Dr. King, it's Dr. Juarez. I have a 47-year-old healthy male; last name Carpenter; who presented with 24 hours of diffuse abdominal pain and fever. He was tender in his right lower abdomen but no guarding or rebound. He had a white count of 14,000 and CT of the belly that showed appendicitis without rupture. I gave him two liters of saline, Dilaudid, and a dose of Zosyn. He is stable. I spoke with Dr. Sellars, who is on for surgery, and he said he prefers that he be admitted to your service for medical evaluation, but he plans to go to the OR around 5 p.m. The patient has been NPO since 8 a.m. Anything else I can do for you on this case? Sure, I will see you down here in a few minutes. Thank you for the timely call back."

Patients want:

- A basic explanation of diagnosis and why the treatment plan warrants further inpatient care.
- A sense of how long the ED/inpatient transition will take.

- The ability to trust the next provider (i.e., hospitalist) as if they are a surrogate for their primary care doctor while in the hospital.
- Seamless information sharing and continuity of care with the next provider (i.e., hospitalist) and ongoing comfort care.

Here's an example of what it sounds like when the ED physician meets the patient's needs well as she's being admitted from the ED to the inpatient unit:

"Mrs. Campbell, I want to go over the testing and treatment that we did today and let you know the game plan. Is your pain okay right now? The blood tests and x-ray have returned, and the good news is that there is no sign of heart damage. If you recall, though, I told you earlier that given your age, the abnormal ECG, and your pain relief with that nitro pill, that I would plan on admitting you overnight to rule out a heart blockage as a cause of your discomfort.

"You are stable, though, and you are in the right place. We have an excellent hospitalist, Dr. Hakim, who will be admitting you for further testing. The hospitalist is an extension of your family doctor, who doesn't admit here.

"Rest assured, I have passed all the important information about you to the admitting hospitalist, and he has given orders for your continued care on Telemetry. What questions can I answer?

"Time-wise, we are looking at approximately two hours before you leave the ED to go up to Telemetry. Should you need the phone, a blanket, a trip to the bathroom, or a snack, just hit this call light and Jill will be over to take care of you. Hang in there; you are doing fine…and I am on shift until 10 p.m. if you need me."

Align Goals to Drive Effective Hospitalist Collaboration

As one of Studer Group's most popular ED speakers and coaches, Wolf Schynoll, MD, FACEP, shares in his recent white paper, the key to driving collaboration and performance is aligning and cascading goals between the ED physician, hospitalist, ED manager, and inpatient manager. (Download a copy of Dr. Schynoll's *Best Practices for Patient Safety: How to Drive Collaboration between Emergency Department Physicians and Hospitalists for Strong Organizational Performance* at www.FireStarterPublishing.com / AdvanceYourED.)

As Dr. Schynoll explains, "The reality is we are all dependent upon each other to promote and facilitate quality clinical outcomes and ensure patient safety. Just as ED physicians request that hospitalists respond to pages in a timely manner, hospitalists desire ED physicians to call them at the appropriate time so they can determine the type of bed needed for the patient and plan their bedside assessment accordingly."

When *is* the best time for the ED physician to call the hospitalist? It's the time that all stakeholders agree upon by defining and tracking it. While one hospitalist might prefer that all labs be back before the ED calls, another might prefer early admissions planning. But when all stakeholders define organization-wide guidelines together—to supersede individual preferences—we raise the standard of care for all patients.

Here's what goal alignment looks like for two sample goals that the ED shares with the hospitalist:

Figure 8.1

Sample Hospital Goals: Improve Throughput for Admitted Patients; Improve HCAHPS Results- 9s/10s

ED Physician Goal	Hospitalist Goal	ED Manager Goal	Inpatient Manager Goal
Disposition to Admitted time: median 138 mins*	Disposition to Admitted time: median 138 mins	Disposition to Admitted time: median 138 mins	Disposition to Admitted time: median 138 mins
Tactics:			
• Page hospitalist at the agreed upon stage of patient work-up. • Write timely transition orders.	• Respond to ED page within 20 minutes. • Adhere to guidelines on coming to ED to see patients.	• Ensure transporters are available within 10 minutes of notification. • Call timely patient reports to floor.	• Accept patient within 15 minutes of notification of bed available and patient accepted by hospitalist. • Accept ED nursing report in timely manner.

* Note: Disposition-to-admitted time of 138 minutes is the national median as noted in Premier's 2006 report "Emergency Department and Best Practices: A Report of the Premier ED Survey Findings."

To be successful, the group's aligned patient care practice policies must translate to greater patient safety and promote collaboration between ED and hospitalist physicians. A tip: In our experience, this is best achieved through transparent data, ideally at the individual provider level as outlined in Chapter 6.

Bryan Medical Center Aligns Goals for Collaboration

"We're using Leader Evaluation Manager® to align goals to improve hospital-wide collaboration for more efficient patient flow," explains John Woodrich, president and COO of Bryan Medical Center in Lincoln, NE. "ED managers, the ED director, administrative managers, and the nursing director over the house supervisors each have goals weighted 25 percent of their evaluations on flow metrics they can impact."

Until recently, all nursing units except for the ED were reporting to the CNO. But when the CNO position opened up recently, the medical center elected to move the ED under the new CNO for even more alignment. When senior leaders brought all stakeholders together for a first meeting on how to improve the ED-to-inpatient transition for patients, this high-performing group reviewed data and quickly identified key processes—not people—as the reason for delays.

As is the case in most hospitals, too much time was elapsing from when ED physicians notified hospitalists about an inpatient admission to when the patient transfer could occur. The administrative managers had to scramble to determine whether they were waiting on an available bed, whether the floor was staffed to accept the patient, or whether housekeeping had cleared the room.

ED physicians explained that within the first 10 minutes of seeing a patient they could determine with about 90 percent accuracy whether or not the patient would need to be admitted. As a result, the medical center added an icon in the electronic physician order entry system that physicians could use at the beginning of the patient visit to note patient diagnosis, what type of bed would likely be needed, and approximate time until the patient would leave the ED. Now administrative managers can align resources quickly for less patient wait time. Attending physicians on inpatient floors can also quickly access the patient's electronic record with another icon added.

"We've had only three monthly stakeholder meetings so far," adds Woodrich, "but the payoffs have already been huge in driving process improvement for better patient care. It's been impressive teamwork."

Use Stakeholder Meetings to Define and Track Progress

Use monthly stakeholder meetings as outlined earlier to first set agreed upon operational metrics and then to review performance to those goals among all stakeholders for effective ED-hospitalist collaboration.

Studer Group recommends that stakeholders develop a shared monthly dashboard that includes metrics for which all stakeholders are accountable. (See sample in Chapter 2.) These metrics are then tracked and reported in a dashboard format at the regularly scheduled stakeholder meeting.

Disposition-to-admitted time (e.g., "ED admit time to head in the bed") is a great metric to include, because you can quickly determine where the bottlenecks are in the admissions process. It facilitates a discussion about the quickest way of getting patients admitted to improve safety, and ensures that the expectations you've agreed upon are met.

While it's key that physician leaders attend the meetings, the group will also benefit from more robust dialogue on what's working well or not working when frontline physicians attend. Nobody wants extra meetings so be creative about how you hardwire these monthly stakeholder meetings. Some organizations, for instance, will rotate forums, having one or two hospitalists with their leader attend a regularly scheduled ED meeting on an every-other-month basis and then have ED physicians attend a scheduled hospitalist meeting during the other months.

Other organizations have used their monthly stakeholder meetings to define clinical pathways or processes. Perhaps the hospitalist prefers that a cardiologist be called on every chest pain rule out, recognizing that ED physicians don't typically consult a cardiologist on every low-risk chest pain case. The hospitalist may explain that it is difficult to secure a cardiologist after admission and therefore prefer early involvement of the cardiologist. The meeting offers an opportunity to promote a common pathway for higher clinical quality and efficiency.

Another way many hospitals use stakeholder meetings is as a forum to establish key criteria for cases that trigger a review because they are mutually inclusive of the ED and hospital stakeholders. The goal is to enhance—not duplicate—reviews by a quality review officer. (That officer should be included in the review of such cases.)

By beginning with a review of the metrics established on the dashboard, it's a natural segue into identifying trends for improvement in individual cases. Some examples of potential triggers for review: delay in the hospitalist seeing the patient of greater than four hours after admission; patient discharges from the inpatient unit within 12 to 24 hours; cases where the patient was transferred to a higher level of care within 12 hours; and 30-day readmits.

The group can examine cases where unnecessary delays put the patient at risk; cases where the work-up of the patient in the ED led to unanticipated clinical issues; and cases where something unanticipated happened due to miscommunications between the ED physician and hospitalist.

Establishing Transition Orders for Admitted Patients

Increasingly, we find that many organizations across the country have implemented transition orders for ED admitted patients if real-time orders cannot be obtained from the admitting physicians. They offer a safe and effective means of transitioning care from the ED to the floors. We support the American College of Emergency Physicians' (ACEP) position that bridge orders should be a short-term solution for safely caring for patients. It's a practical solution to ensure timely clinical care between the time the patient arrives to the floor and the actual time until the attending physician arrives to see the patient.

However, there should be a clear expectation between the ED and admitting physician about the appropriate length of time that it takes to transition care from one physician to the next. Bridge orders are time-bound and should state an expiration time. In fact, expiration of transition orders should be tracked as a key element on your dashboard as such cases indicate an opportunity for process improvement. Individual provider data on this metric is essential.

So in summary, we find there are three main tools that are most effective for promoting the quality of this important handoff. First, use stakeholder meetings for all the reasons we've discussed. It hardwires an opportunity for both the ED and the hospitalist to recognize that they are, in fact, each other's internal customers and drive a shared agenda. When you understand the other physician as your customer, you ask, "What can I do for you? How can we be more efficient?" Both groups can provide input and celebrate the wins.

Second, use AIDET to promote positive handoffs and manage up the receiving physician. When you assure patients that you are handing them off to a well-qualified physician, you reduce patient anxiety and improve patient perception of care. You build the patient's trust and confidence, setting up the next provider for success.

And third, we recommend physician leader rounding on both physicians and patients. This is the accountability piece. It is a simple way for leaders to validate that our actions are achieving the desired result. As the ED-hospitalist team rolls out process improvements, physician leaders actively track how well things are working for both physicians and patients by asking what's going well, harvesting wins, and identifying further opportunities for process improvements. The best practice is to hardwire it by using the appropriate rounding logs. (Download three samples at www. FireStarterPublishing.com/AdvanceYourED.)

The result? Improved clinical outcomes, more efficient throughput for admitted patients, and higher organizational performance.

Again, the ED-hospitalist transition is a critical handover in healthcare delivery. It can have a serious impact on clinical outcomes as well as the patient's perception of his or her entire stay. By understanding the primary needs of all three parties, and making sure the ED physician and hospitalist collaborate as a team, we will meet our mission of delivering the highest clinical quality while maintaining best-in-class communication in a compassionate and caring way.

Key Learning Points: Driving Collaboration within the Hospital

1. Hardwire twice-daily bed flow meetings if you haven't already done so. They are a natural extension of the monthly stakeholder meetings and ED pre-shift huddles you're already using for real-time information to ensure quality patient care.

2. To close performance gaps, engage physicians in collaboration early—use stakeholder meetings—when rolling out new tools and tactics. Always begin by communicating the evidence for why new behaviors are good for patients and quality outcomes. Show them how powerful their role modeling of collaboration can be in changing the entire culture of the organization.

3. Drive collaboration with hospitalists by first understanding the needs of both physicians and patients during the handoff from ED to inpatient units. Then align and cascade goals with key metrics (e.g., disposition-to-admit time) to track individual accountability.

4. Establish transition orders for admitted patients. Bridge orders should be a short-term solution for safely caring for patients during likely time delays between when the patient arrives to the floor and the actual time until the attending physician arrives to see the patient. They should be time-limited.

5. Use physician leader rounding on both physicians and patients to validate actions are achieving desired results.

CHAPTER 9

Driving Collaboration within the Community

"I can do all things through Him who gives me strength."
—*Philippians 4:13*

One of the most important things we can do to ensure quality care for patients in the ED and reduce inappropriate utilization is to collaborate effectively with other providers in the community.

For example, emergency medical services (EMS) is a group that can significantly impact an ED's reputation, volume, and quality. EMS providers practice in a difficult environment where immediate decisions are made on a regular basis and the stakes are high. When EMS personnel arrive in the ED, it's important that providers support them, listen, and help them offload patients efficiently.

Manage up what they have done well (e.g., "Great job on this resuscitation," or, "You were right on target calling this acute MI"). If there's an opportunity for improvement, frame it as an "educational moment" and help them learn so we can positively impact similar future cases together. Recognition goes a long way to building collaboration. (In fact, consider catering lunch in the EMS room—complete with appreciation banners—on National EMS Appreciation Day!)

You can also partner with EMS to drive clinical quality by forming a clinical case board. It works like this: Focus on a clinical area that is positively impacted by aligned and streamlined processes from EMS to ED, such as acute myocardial infarction. Cite the cases for a given month.

If you're focusing on acute MIs, as in this example, you'd follow up on compliance for aspirin administration, pre-hospital ECG, successful transport to the ED, time to cath lab activation, and door-to-balloon time. By reviewing these performance metrics with ED personnel, EMS teams up with the ED for a dramatic impact on quality care from the street to the hospital gurney to the patient's discharge.

Assessing and Treating Super Users

One of the most frequent questions we hear as we speak and coach EDs on driving excellence is: "What can we do about super users?" The long-term solution to ensuring these patients are treated in more appropriate settings is through collaboration with primary care and other specialty providers in the community as we'll discuss below, but there are also some effective approaches you can begin using right now.

Super users define a group of individuals who over-frequent the ED. They encompass several groups of patients. First, there are those ESI level 4 to 5 patients who don't have access to a primary care provider, prefer the convenience of the ED (because the ED's Fast Track outperforms the local urgent care clinic, for example), or are uninsured.

According to a May 2012 report[34] by *HealthLeaders Media*, 85 percent of 298 ED leader respondents predicted an increase in the number of uninsured patients over the coming year. Forty-two percent of respondents predicted that healthcare reform will have a negative impact on the ED in terms of patient volume, and 78 percent predicted it would have a negative impact in terms of ED reimbursement.

In addition, there are 50 million chronic pain patients in the U.S. today. Let's pause to consider that number for a moment.

50,000,000

estimated U.S. chronic pain patients

Not only that, but the Centers for Disease Control and Prevention and the Substance Abuse and Mental Health Services Administration cite a doubling of misuses/overdose cases presenting to EDs between 2004 and 2008 for a total of 1 million cases.[35] That is the same estimated ED caseload for illicit drug abuse. And yet, according to that same 2012 *HealthLeaders* study, only one third of respondents said they have programs in place that focus on specific conditions to divert patients from the ED!

Figure 9.1
Meds Gone Wrong

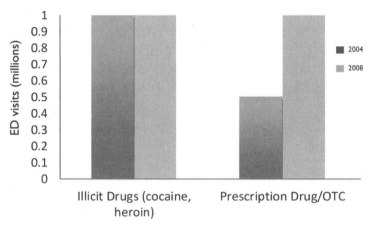

While ED cases for illicit drugs have remained stable from 2004 to 2008, prescription drug abuse has doubled in five years and is on the rise compared to street drugs. In fact, estimated ED visits for non-medical opioid use have increased 111 percent while visits for non-medical benzodiazepine use have increased 89 percent.

It is no wonder that with volumes higher than ever, ED providers feel resentful and frustrated that super users take a disproportionate amount of time and resources away from patients with acute, emergent conditions when they should be seeking care from primary care providers and specialists in the community. Worst of all, abusive "drug-seeking" patients can completely drain us of our sense of purpose, worthwhile work, and making a difference with irrational and combative demands for controlled substances.

But this may be a surprise to you: **Studer Group research from our national ED learning lab shows that on average, patients with true drug-seeking behaviors comprise just 3 percent of ED volume!**

While increasing volumes are a real issue due to the issues noted above, it's also important for ED staff and providers to do a bit of a reality check when it comes to the problem of dealing with true drug seekers. While nearly every ED seems to feel this is a problem unique to their own ED, the truth is that nearly all regions of the United States share this challenge. (Internationally, the same problem exists, but frequently with slightly different medications in the opioid, benzodiazepine, or muscle relaxation categories.)

Frequently, providers will blame poor patient perception of care on their refusal to prescribe medications to these patients. But the reality is, they make up such a small percentage of your ED patient population that you will increase overall patient perception of care—and move your ED from good to great—by focusing on pain, plan of care, and duration as we've discussed earlier, for *all* patients.

Another thing to consider: If your ED is focused on shifting more patients' perception of care to "excellent," which group of patients would be more likely to move? ED consumers who already rate the care as "good" or those who rate care as "very poor"? Patients who cite the care as "good" are happy and satisfied. More attention to effective communications and operations will move their perception of care to the top box, so focus there!

Figure 9.2
Super Users Defined

Overuse for ESI
4-5 Care

Legitimate Chronic
Painful Conditions

Suspicious Painful
Conditions

ED super users are comprised of three groups: those who overuse the ED due to convenience; those with legitimate chronic conditions; and those with suspicious painful conditions.

Drug Seeker or Legitimate Medical Issue?

A patient who is fraudulent and drug-seeking is someone who seems more interested in the medicine itself than the relief of pain, while a patient with legitimate, authentic symptoms is likely to adopt an attitude of "I don't care what you do! Please just help me get rid of this pain!"[36]

Other clues that you are dealing with a true drug-seeking patient include specific requests for narcotics, previous documented visits for suspected drug-seeking, unwillingness to try simple analgesia, or aggressive/demanding behaviors.[37]

Treatment Issues and Risks

Emergency physicians are stewards of the Hippocratic Oath ("Do no harm."). For the drug seeker, it's critical that we assess the overdose potential. We're reminded of this responsibility each time we read about a tragic, high-profile celebrity death. Medication toxicity, changes in the type of medication given, and large variations in management all present significant risks for drug seekers.

We cannot prescribe in such a way that worsens a chronic addiction or enable variance in medication use and dosing. While Dr. Johnson might be resolute in her non-prescribing, Dr. Brown might give in on the next visit because he feels so uncomfortable with the whole situation. Maybe he doesn't want to irritate or inflame a patient so that they disrupt the ED or complain to administrators or licensing agencies. But what message does this send about the consistency of your ED?

Drug-seeking behavior is a complex health issue. It's a multi-factorial problem that ultimately requires multi-disciplinary management (e.g., psychotherapy, counseling, and organized pain management). So the ED is clearly not the best or most appropriate setting for these patients to receive care.

However, some patients who present as suspicious "drug seekers" may not be abusing drugs. **Remember that pain is the most common reason a patient visits an ED!** Perhaps the patient is physiologically dependent on medication he's been taking as prescribed (e.g., a patient with multiple back surgeries who was prescribed opiates, but is suffering with chronic, breakthrough pain). Remember that back pain is the second most common reason for absenteeism from work after the common cold and it is the most common capacity-limiting ailment.

On the other hand, maybe the individual *is* a drug seeker, but also has a legitimate acute condition.

Here's what such ED patients say after a poor encounter:

- "I could tell the doctor thought I was here for drugs."
- "She wouldn't even listen once she knew I had been here before."
- "Do you really think that I like to go to the ED?"
- "I have no insurance. Where else am I supposed to go for this pain?"
- "That doctor labeled me from the minute he walked in."

That's why it's critical that providers perform a complete and thorough medical history and exam. In fact, we have an obligation under the Emergency Medical Treatment and Active Labor Act (EMTALA) to medically screen and examine all patients who present in the ED, even those whom we suspect are drug-seeking. Studer Group recommends that providers set aside any preconceived notions during this history and exam until they've collected all available information to exclude an emergency medical condition.

Otherwise, the ED team risks missing important history and physical exam findings, medicating illegitimate patients, or avoiding the prescription of medication for those with legitimate pain. Providers may develop a poor attitude or indifference to cases that seem suspicious, but may be legitimate, unfairly stigmatizing such patients. This then creates risk and poor perception of care.

Best Practices in Managing True Drug Seekers

One useful emerging tool that many Emergency Departments are using to manage these individuals is statewide surveillance systems. ED physicians can access them to track the frequency and types of prescriptions suspicious patients are filling at pharmacies statewide. For example, one study from the *Annals of Emergency Medicine* reported that 41 percent of providers altered their prescribing practice after accessing the Ohio Automated Rx Reporting System (OARRS).[38]

Another best practice is to *always* respect a patient's privacy and dignity. Be methodical. Listen and leave your emotions behind. Also, have a game plan for what can be offered while avoiding comments like "There's nothing we can do for you," which only escalates the conflict. Also, set limits or boundaries and disclose these up-front. AIDET is extremely useful in these provider-patient interactions because it demonstrates care and compassion and also offers an opportunity to link the patient with community resources that are better suited to address the issue than the ED.

At Studer Group, we've found AIDET to be an effective tool to quickly diffuse potential confrontations and gain patient compliance with provider treatment plans at EDs in our national learning lab.

Here is an example of how it might sound:

A—Acknowledge:
"Good morning, Mr. Faber, can I come in?"
(Ensures you are speaking with the correct patient, no negative opening lines.)

I—Introduce:
"I'm Dr. Roberts, one of the emergency physicians here at XYZ Hospital." *(Offers handshake and eye contact.)* "I have practiced for 13 years. I understand you are here for continued back pain."
(Introduces self and role and further acknowledges their presenting illness.)

D—Duration:
"Tell me more about this medical problem and then I will examine you. This should take only about five minutes."
(History is completed with documentation of chronicity, level of pain,

any new neurological deficits, comparison to prior episodes, and current pain management strategy. Physical exam documents subjective distress level, muscle strength, sensation, reflexes, and back exam.) **(Patient's concern is taken seriously and documented appropriately.)**

E—Explanation:
"Mr. Faber, based on your exam, history, and medical record review, you are presenting again for chronic back pain. Because I care about your total health and must abide by our system's chronic pain policy, I don't believe that further prescription of these habit-forming medications is in your best interest. I would like to offer you a steroid injection to reduce inflammation and a resource list of several outpatient clinics where you can enroll in a chronic pain management program and receive continuity of care. We know from the medical literature that patients with your condition will experience fewer episodes of pain and less variation of care with this approach." **(Answers patient questions.)**

(This approach allows for prudent medical management. This patient feels he was taken seriously and was not demeaned. The provider also tied together all the information and findings in an objective and cordial way, offered real-time means to deal with pain, offered further resources for outpatient care, and clearly stated his rationale for non-narcotic prescribing).

T—Thank you:
"Mr. Faber, I hope this makes sense and we thank you for complying with the treatment plan. I wish you the best."
(Overall sense that you did "care" within the constraints of prescribing and the pain policy. Non-punitive perception by patient.)

For the majority of such patients, Studer Group finds this approach to be very effective in diffusing a potentially difficult interaction. Are you uncomfortable with the idea of "thanking" these patients? Please don't be. You are not thanking them for coming to your ED with the chronic pain. Rather, you are thanking them for complying with your treatment plan, which frequently diffuses further objections.

The reason that AIDET works so well is because it sets a tone of caring, reduces anxiety, and demonstrates that you are non-judgmental, open-minded, and objective. When a patient perceives a provider in that way, he will calm down and comply with the treatment decision in about 80 percent of cases. When a provider does not use AIDET, she may leave a patient misinformed or with the perception that she doesn't have time for or interest in him. All patients may not need narcotic medications, but all patients deserve our care, dignity, and respect.

However, if, in spite of well-executed AIDET, the patient refuses to accept a provider's treatment decision, you can use key words such as:

"Mr. Faber, because our mission is to provide prudent care to you and to do no harm, it would be at odds with our commitment to prescribe you more Vicodin. I will prescribe you a medicine that will get at the root of your pain, though—as I explained. Those outpatient resources I shared with you will be very useful in designing a continued care plan for your condition."

When you must prescribe, always prescribe a limited quantity (8 to 15 pills) with no refill. If providing a written script, add a notation: "must fill the antibiotic to receive the pain medication" in cases where an infection is the cause of pain, such as in the case of a dental infection.

The Long-Term Solution: Implement a Chronic Pain Policy

Long-term, **to reduce these unnecessary visits and encourage treatment in more appropriate settings for both drug seekers and other ED super users, the solution is the same: to implement a chronic pain policy that all staff follow consistently.** The policy can include things like what defines drug-seeking behaviors and how to enroll ED "super users" in the ED's chronic pain program. To ensure that ED providers are consistent in their approach to every patient every time, training on both AIDET and the pain policy is crucial.

In Studer Group's popular white paper *Managing Drug-Seeking Behaviors & Super Users in the Emergency Department*, we explain that, essentially, there are several foundational components to implementing an effective pain policy:

- Developing the pain management policy.
- Forming an ED pain committee to screen prospective patients for enrollment.
- Notifying enrolled patients.
- Collaborating with primary care providers (PCPs) or chronic pain management physicians on pain management contracts for patients.
- Communicating with enrolled patients.

"EDs that are most effective at hardwiring a pain management policy implement both a set of clinical guidelines and an enrollment process for managing these types of patients," explains Studer Group ED coach and speaker Wolf Schynoll, MD, FACEP. "For example, the process advocates sending a letter to the patient's PCP on their intent to enroll a patient in the pain management program and also provide a letter to the patient explaining the ED's pain management policy. The objective is to be consistent and prescriptive with both the patient and the PCP to ensure appropriate, quality care in the patient's best interest."

To download a copy of *Managing Drug-Seeking Behaviors & Super Users in the Emergency Department*, visit www.FireStarterPublishing.com/AdvanceYourED.

EmCare Reduces Door-to-Pain Time with Pain Care Policy

In just one month, Tanveer Gaibi, MD, FACEP, EmCare's site medical director and chief of emergency medicine at Northwest Hospital in Randallstown, MD, reduced door-to-pain time for patients from 90 to 60 minutes after implementing an effective pain protocol.

"After we received approval from the hospital's attorney and medical executive committee, we actively engaged MDs and nurses in being more proactive in ordering pain medication," explains Dr. Gaibi. "We also created a diverse super user committee to review random patient cases." The team, which includes the site medical director, RN director, patient representative, case manager, director of inpatient services, and vice president of the Emergency Department, audits patient charts during the meeting to identify super users. The case manager then follows up with patients, their primary care providers, and previous case managers for alignment on a treatment plan.

"We have a high population of sickle cell patients," adds Dr. Gaibi. One such patient claimed she was refused pain medications by her previous primary care provider. When the case manager contacted a pain specialist to collaborate on a pain management plan, the site medical director could intervene directly next time the patient arrived in the ED to ensure better compliance. "We've noticed the staff feels better about the care we provide to this patient population since we've provided education about our pain policy," Dr. Gaibi notes. "And providers feel they are supported by the policy when explaining pain management options to patients."

Step 1: Develop and Implement a Pain Management Policy

An effective pain management policy includes operational guidelines and a process to ensure the appropriate identification of super users, sets a threshold number of ED visits annually, explains the policy to the patient at the bedside, and communicates the desire to enroll the patient into the policy with the patient's PCP. If the patient has no PCP, the pain committee will provide outpatient providers whom the patient can see.

First, the ED must decide what constitutes over-utilization. Some EDs have adapted a definition of four or more visits per month. Others choose six to eight visits per year as a threshold. (Criteria may vary, but each ED or urgent care practice should define what utilization threshold triggers inclusion into the pain management policy and never includes visits for legitimate illnesses or injury.)

Step 2: Form an ED Pain Committee

Once the pain management policy is in place, potential enroll-ees are flagged during an ED visit (after a provider recognizes a suspicious and frequent pattern) and a request for review is made to the ED pain committee. Typically, the committee includes the ED medical director, staff ED physician(s), ED nurse manager(s), pain management doctor (anesthesia or PM&R), administrative leader, chaplain, and case manager. This committee receives and reviews requests on a monthly basis for a yes/no enrollment decision.

Figure 9.3
Process for Enrollment in Chronic Pain Program

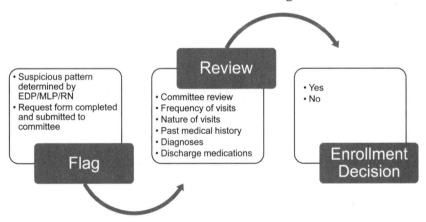

After a patient is enrolled into the plan, an identification pro-cess needs to be implemented to flag the patient as a "super user" the next time they present. For example, this might involve adding a folder to the electronic health record that denotes chronic pain committee review. The folder would contain the letter that was mailed to the patient and the committee's recommendations.

Step 3: Notify Enrolled Super User Patients

Next, the patient is sent a letter stating that a review of his visits has determined he frequents the ED due to a chronic pain condition. While the letter reinforces the willingness of ED providers to see the patient in the future for evaluation and medical screenings to exclude emergency medical conditions, it also asks the patient to schedule an appointment with his PCP or chronic pain management provider to discuss a pain contract that will outline the PCP's treatment plan and allowable visits to better coordinate care.

The letter emphasizes that narcotics will not be included in ED treatment for chronic pain conditions until the PCP has returned the pain contract. (Note: Patients who do not have a primary care physician are asked to establish one, and given suggestions for on-call physicians if needed.) A copy of this letter is included in the patient's medical record as reviewed above.

Step 4: Send the PCP the Patient's Pain Contract Letter

At the same time the patient is notified about his enrollment in the plan, the ED physician sends the patient's PCP a letter communicating that because the PCP's patient is over-utilizing the ED, the ED would like to work with the PCP to create an effective strategy to manage the patient's pain—and align ED care with the PCP's treatment—through the use of a pain management contract. The letter requests that the PCP return the pain management contract to the ED where it will be kept on file to be referenced when the patient visits.

The pain contract form asks the PCP to specify the number of allowed ED/urgent care monthly visits and identify preferred treatments for specific chronic pain conditions. The PCP should discuss the contract with the patient before returning it to the ED. If the completed pain contract allows for too many future ED visits, then the ED medical director will need to dialogue with the physician to negotiate a compromise.

Step 5: Communicate with Enrolled Patients in the ED

Each time a chronic pain patient presents to the ED or urgent care clinic for chronic pain, the ED physician reviews with them the pain contract details. All providers agree to adhere to the pain contract that the PCP has developed. If a patient presents for chronic pain and he has already exceeded his monthly allotted visits for outlined treatment, alternative treatment in the form of non-narcotic medications will be offered.

The overall success in effectively managing chronic pain patients and those exhibiting drug-seeking behavior (to reduce their over-utilization of the ED) depends on all providers consistently adhering to the agreed upon pain management policy.

As noted earlier, it is sometimes hard for providers to have these difficult conversations with such patients, and the easy choice is to give in to their requests. Therefore, it is important to track policy compliance, ensure they are trained on how to use AIDET, develop a strategy to identify providers who deviate from policy, and devise a plan to hold them accountable.

To download a free sample letter from an ED physician to a PCP, patient letter on ED pain management policy, and sample pain contract plan, visit www.FireStarterPublishing.com/AdvanceYourED. (In Appendix B to this downloadable document, you can also review examples of effective key words for managing both first-time and frequent visitors to the ED who are exhibiting drug-seeking behaviors. These are examples of actual dialogue practiced by several of Studer Group's emergency physicians, representing over 35 years of clinical practice.)

In Studer Group's experience, Emergency Departments and urgent care facilities that hardwire a protocol like the one above experience fewer patient complaints and reduced visits from these two patient populations.

In the end, whether we are working to better understand the needs and challenges of emergency medicine service providers for acute patients or are hardwiring communication with primary care providers for patients with chronic pain, the results are the same. Through our commitment to effective collaboration, we extend our impact beyond the walls of the hospital to live our mission by ensuring quality patient care in our communities.

Key Learning Points: Driving Collaboration within the Community

1. Collaboration with EMS is critical to the reputation and quality of an ED. EMS personnel and leadership need to know that they are appreciated and respected and that what they do impacts clinical quality.

2. Super users are those who over-frequent the ED. They include several groups of patients: low-acuity patients who prefer the ED to more appropriate care settings (e.g., no primary care provider or insurance), chronic pain patients, and those with drug-seeking behaviors.

3. "Drug seekers" actually comprise only 3 percent of volume in a typical ED, but are among the most frustrating patients to treat. However, ED providers have a professional obligation to set aside preconceived notions, act respectfully, and perform a thorough medical examination in suspicious cases.

4. Two best practices in managing true drug seekers are accessing statewide surveillance systems and using AIDET to gain patient compliance and avoid confrontations around treatment decisions.

5. The long-term solution for treating super users is to implement an effective chronic pain policy that defines allowable visits, enrolls super users, notifies patients, and requires a completed pain contract from the patient's PCP, which is reviewed with the patient when presenting in the ED.

Embracing Change: Have a Great Day Every Day

In Studer Group's first ED book, *Excellence in the Emergency Department: How to Get Results*, which was published in 2009, we talked about the rapid pace of change. Now, three years later, change continues to *accelerate*, and pressures are yet *greater* due to increasing volumes, reform, transparency, and reimbursement changes. In fact, we predict that in five years, we will think of these as the good old days!

The reality is that change is not going away. While we can collaborate with other providers in the community to move some patients to more appropriate care settings, an ever-increasing number of patients will view the ED as their "safety net." For many, it's the only form of healthcare they will ever have.

The good news—then, as now—is that we can do this! We are "can-do" people. If you've read this far, you now have even more tools you can start using today to meet these challenges and make your ED a great place for physicians to practice, employees to work, and patients to receive care. You've read lots of evidence on exactly why these work so well and heard from ED leaders nationwide about their positive and dramatic impact.

But here's the bottom line: Someday, you or someone you love is going to be in that bed. Some day, the life you save might be your own. Now is our time in the ED to make a critical difference in the patient experience.

What does a great day in the ED look like from a patient perspective? You'll hear patient comments like "Wow! I can't believe how fast I got in!" or "The doctor started my treatment right away, managed my pain, and kept me informed about what was going to happen next the whole time I was there. It was such a relief!" You'll see patients visibly relax as they understand, through your actions—like AIDET, quick triage, and proactive communication—that they're in good hands. Then they'll be wowed by that post-visit phone call. They'll feel like you *really* care...which is so important, because of course you care!

You know, if you're working in the ED, you can have a terrible day seeing just 100 patients if processes aren't working or the CT scanner is down. Or, you can have a fabulous day seeing 180 patients when flow is efficient and a high-performing team is turning that flywheel. In EDs like these, absenteeism is low. Staff want to come to work because their contributions feel meaningful. They feel valued and recognized every day.

When your ED is operating efficiently, processes work well. When providers and staff are communicating effectively, patients are receiving timely, quality care. When everyone is collaborating consistently, you'll hear staff comments like "X-ray was great today," "Lab was really turning patients around for us," and "We got to take our lunch break even though we had so many patients." You'll stop hearing about everyone's frustrations during your pre-shift huddles and start hearing about all the wins. New staff will feel included and informed, instead of feeling left out. In short, your team will be grateful.

As absenteeism drops off and you retain a high-performing staff, your providers will notice...and they too will begin to have some great days in the ED. Instead of asking questions of temporary nurses distracted by their smartphones who don't know how a doctor's patient is doing, physicians will feel relieved to be working with a high-performing, talented retained workforce...individuals who anticipate their needs and communicate proactively.

They'll love the fact that they can diagnose, treat, and disposition patients quickly because flow is efficient and tech support for labs and x-ray is timely. Just like high-performing staff, good physicians *want* to see patients all day long. They just don't want angry patients who are waiting for consults, labs, or the hospitalist to show up.

In the end, no matter where we work in the ED, we all want the same thing. We want to feel confident we've delivered timely, quality care. We want to see that patient who arrived anxious and in pain leave feeling grateful and on the road to recovery...because that's what we signed up for in emergency medicine.

That's why your ability to adopt a positive attitude, take swift action, and implement new leadership behaviors is so important. In fact, it's mission critical! That's our mission in emergency medicine: to save lives and restore health. If not you, who?

Acknowledgments

Together, the authors would like to thank the following key individuals at Studer Group: Quint Studer, for your unwavering vision and commitment to improve healthcare, your boundless passion to enhance quality, and your remarkable ability to accelerate needed change. We are each grateful for your ongoing mentorship and coaching. BG Porter, for your active support of our ED work, and for being a consistent role model to all of us at Studer Group for what true leadership is. You are what "right" looks like. Bekki Kennedy, for providing guidance and direction in navigating this journey, for reducing our anxiety as deadlines approached, and for believing in us always. We are each so grateful to you. Chris Román, for being brave enough to take on this project with three authors, and for keeping us all consistently on course throughout this process. Thank you for editing the book multiple times and offering your expert advice and knowledge along the way. You are simply the best!

I would like to thank Barbara Hotko for her wise and consistent mentorship, her exceptional passion, her relentless pursuit of excellence, and her invaluable friendship. Hottie, I am filled with gratitude to have you as a constant in my life. Blessings on you and Dan. Stacy Tompkins, for your clear insight, your ability to handle any and all situations with grace, your unmatched attentiveness to our partners, and for always giving it to me straight! I couldn't do it without you. Lynne Cunningham, for your ongoing friendship and counsel, and for always having a good answer when I don't. You never cease to amaze me! My coauthors of this book, Regina Shupe and Dan Smith, for your relentless pursuit of excellence... always. Faye Sullivan, for your never-ending help in improving the quality and consistency of our ED coaching materials. The ED coaching team, for your tireless efforts to improve ED performance. The entire Studer Group family, for your support, friendship, and steadfast commitment to our mission, vision, and values. My partners, for the opportunity to work with such wonderful, diverse organizations and such passionate and inspired leaders. My aunt and uncle, Paul and Roberta Pratt, for your unconditional love and support throughout my life's ups and downs. You are my steadfast rock. The Williams and Baker families, for your love and prayers, and for helping me "hardwire" my values to keep God first and family second, always.

—Stephanie Baker, RN, CEN, MBA

I would like to thank each of my many uncles, aunts, and cousins for their lifelong love and unconditional support. You have given me the courage to do the work that I do. Dan Collard, for being the first to ignite my passion to become both a better leader myself and to inspire leadership excellence in others. It is because of you that I am able to serve as a change agent in this country today. Julie Kennedy, for your astute guidance and mentorship through the years. Your passion and commitment to excellence in healthcare have fueled my own desire to help create the work environments we both wish for our daughters as future nurses. Kelly Dickey, my friend, coworker, and overall go-to girl. I am grateful daily for your tremendous skill that, in turn, allows me to better serve our partners. Stephanie Baker, Dan Smith, Faye Sullivan, and the ED team at Studer Group, thank you for the opportunity to work in a field I truly love and mentoring me to be my best. My Studer Group coaching family, for your tireless work to make healthcare better for physicians, staff, and above all, patients. My partner organizations, for trusting me to share in your journey, ignite your excitement, and take you and your Emergency Departments to peak performance. To all of my coworkers over the last 27 years, because of you, I am the nurse, mentor, and leader that I am today.

—Regina Shupe, RN, MSN, CEN

I would like to express many thanks to ED staff, physicians, and leaders everywhere. You are the "real deal," as the safety net and front door to healthcare and impact countless lives daily. Baptist Health System in San Antonio, TX, my "home" hospital, for trusting me to coach our emergency physicians to top performance when we were deep in the valley. Trip Pilgrim, Graham Reeves, and Kent Wallace: I am so glad to have shared this journey with you. Physicians and leaders at Emergency Physicians' Affiliates, whom I continue to learn from daily. Dr. Jim Potyka and Dr. Tim Taylor, for allowing me to be a part of our fine group and entrusting me to lead our service performance program. Sam Spencer, who sat with me at a table in the hospital, my home, and at many coffee shops to analyze satisfaction data, develop scorecards, and track physician performance. An energetic and bright leader at Baptist, you are also a valued friend. To Studer Group colleagues and leaders, for generously sharing your talents and expertise with me on this incredible journey since 2009. I am grateful for your support and teamwork. This is our time to make a difference! Regina Shupe and Stephanie Baker, for the privilege of speaking, coaching, and writing with you. It is truly my honor to work with you both. Max Lucado, my pastor and friend, for your prayers and encouragement. My wife, Kristen, for your unwavering faith in me and support for my passion and work to make emergency care better. Thanks for all you do to keep the home front humming when I am on the road or seeing patients. You are a blessing.

—Dan Smith, MD, FACEP

Additional Recommended Reading: Articles by Interest Area

Wait Times and Duration in the ED

Walsh, M. et al. "Satisfaction with the ED environment decreases with length of stay." *Ann Emerg Med* 51, no. 4 (2008): 513.

Horwitz, L.I. et al. "US ED performance on wait time and length of visit." *Ann Emerg Med* 55, no. 2 (2010): 133-41.

Bastani, A. et al. "How long before patients lose their patience?" *Ann Emerg Med* 52, no. 4 (2008): 586-7.

Operational/Process/LEAN Improvements for the ED

Dickson, E.W. et al. "Use of LEAN in the ED: A case series of 4 hospitals." *Ann Emerg Med* 54, no. 4 (2009): 504-10.

Wiler, J.L. et al. "Optimizing ED front-end operations." *Ann Emerg Med* 55, no. 2 (2010): 142-60.

Chan, T.C. et al. "Impact of rapid entry and accelerated care at triage on reducing ED patient wait times, lengths of stay and rate of left without being seen." *Ann Emerg Med* 46, no. 6 (2005): 491-7.
Mink, J. et al. "A lean-based process redesign and its impact on patient satisfaction: The SPEED trial." *Ann Emerg Med* 56, no. 3 (2010): S111.

Sayah, A. et al. "ED operational improvements' impact on volume, quality core measures, patient stay and satisfaction." *Ann Emerg Med* 54, no. 3 (2009): S51.

Robinson, K. et al. "An educational pamphlet may improve patient satisfaction in a busy tertiary care ED." *Ann Emerg Med* 51, no. 4 (2008): 543.

Papa, L. et al. "Does preparing for their ED experience through a waiting room video about process of care improve their satisfaction?" *Ann Emerg Med* 46, no. 3 (2005): 23-4.

Jensen, K. "Staffing an ED appropriately and efficiently." *ACEP News*, Aug. 2009.

Scheck, A. "Performance metrics improve ED efficiency." *Emergency Medicine News*, Jan. 2012.

Boarding Solutions

ACEP Task Force Report on Boarding: Emergency Department Overcrowding: High Impact Solutions. Apr. 2008.

Kelen, G.D. et al. "Creation of surge capacity by early discharge of hospitalized patients at low risk for untoward events." *Disaster Med Public Health Prep* 3 (2009): S10.

McManus, M. et al. "Variability in surgical caseload and access to intensive care services." *Anesthesiology* 98 (2003): 1491-6.

Litvak, E. et al. "More Patients, Less Payment: Increasing Hospital Efficiency in the Aftermath of Health Reform." *Health Affairs* 30, no. 1 (2011): 76-80.

Bibliography

Introduction:

1   Niska, R. et. al. "National Hospital Ambulatory Medical Care Survey: 2007 Emergency Department Summary." *National Health Statistics Report* 26 (2010).

2   Ibid.

3   The Center for Medical Education, Inc. "Streamlining admissions." *ED Leadership Monthly* (Nov. 2009).

4   Forero, R. et al. "Access block and ED overcrowding." *Emerg Med Australas* 22, no. 2 (Apr. 2010): 119-35.

5   Kulstad, E.B., and K.M. Kelley. "Overcrowding is associated with Delays in percutaneous coronary intervention for acute myocardial infarction." *Int J Emerg Med.* 2, no. 3 (Jun. 5, 2009): 149-54.

6   Fee, C., E. Weber, C. Maak, and P. Bacchetti. "Effect of emergency department crowding on time to antibiotics in patients admitted with community-acquired pneumonia." *Ann Emerg Med.* 50, no. 5 (Nov. 2007): 501-9.

7   Pitts, S.R., R.W. Niska et al. "National Hospital Ambulatory Medical Care Survey: 2006 Emergency Department Summary." *National Health Stat Report* 7 (Aug. 6, 2008): 1-38.

8   Healthcare Financial Management Association. *Value in Health Care: Current State and Future Directions* (Jun. 2011).

9   "Pulse Report 2010 Emergency Department: Patient Perspectives on American Health Care." South Bend, IN: Press Ganey Associates, Inc., 2010.

10   Ibid.

Chapter 1:

11   Pitts, S. et al. "National Hospital Ambulatory Medical Care Survey: 2006 Emergency Department Summary." *National Health Statistics Reports* no. 7 (Aug. 6, 2008). U.S. Department of Health and Human Services, Center for Disease Control and Prevention.

12   "Consensus Statement: Definitions for Consistent Emergency Department Metrics." *Amer Academy of Emergency Medicine, Amer Academy of Pediatrics, Amer Association of Critical Care Nurses, Amer College of Emergency Physicians, Amer Nurses Association, Association of perioperative Registered Nurses, Emergency Department Practice Management Association, Emergency Nurses Association, National Association of EMS Physicians* (Jul. 2011).

13   Compiled based on best practices identified in:
Health Care Advisory Board (HCAB). *Emergency Department Investment Blueprint*. Washington DC: The Advisory Board Company, 2007.
Clinical Initiatives Center. *The Clock Work ED: Volumes 1-III*. Washington DC: The Advisory Board Company, 1999.
H*Works. "Emergency Department and Capacity Throughput Benchmarks." Washington DC: The Advisory Board Company, 2006.

McGrayne, J. "ED Benchmarks and Best Practices." *VHA* (2005). http://www.iienet2.org/uploadedFiles/SHS/Resource_Library/Details/05_mcgrayne.pdf.

HCAB. *Hospital of the Future*. Washington, DC: The Advisory Board Company, 2007.

Clinical Advisory Board. *Emergency Care Reform: Executive Briefing for Clinical Leaders*. Washington DC: The Advisory Board Company, 2000.

14   Forster, A. et al. "The incidence and severity of adverse events affecting patients after discharge from the hospital." *Annals of Internal Medicine* 138, no. 3 (Feb. 4, 2003): 161-7.

15   Forster, A. et al. "Adverse drug events occurring following hospital discharge." *J Gen Intern Med.* 20, no. 4 (Apr. 2005): 317-23.

16   Studer Alliance for Healthcare Research. "Emergency Department Rounding Study." Gulf Breeze, FL: Studer Group, 2007.

Chapter 3:

17   Walsh, M. et al. "Satisfaction with the ED environment decreases with length of stay." *Ann Emerg Med* 51, no. 4 (2008): 513.

18   Horwitz, L.I. et al. "U.S. ED Performance on Wait Time and Length of Visit." *Ann Emerg Med* 55, no. 2 (2010): 133-41.

19   Report to the Chairman, Committee of Finance, U.S. Senate. *Hospital Emergency Departments: Crowding Continues to Occur, and Some Patients Wait Longer than Recommended Time Frames* (Apr. 2009) GAO-09-347.

20   ACEP Task Force Report on Boarding. *Emergency Department Overcrowding: High Impact Solutions* (Apr. 2008).

21   Schneider, S.M., M.E. Gallery, R. Schafermeyer et al. "Emergency department crowding: a point in time." *Ann Emerg Med.* 42 (2003): 167-72.

22   "Chapter 3: Utilization and Volume." In Chartbook: Trends Affecting Hospitals and Health Systems. Chicago: American Hospital Association, 2010.

23   McManus, M.L., M.C. Long, A. Cooper et al. "Variability in surgical caseload and access to intensive care services." *Anesthesiology* 98 (2003): 1491-6.

24   ACEP Task Force Report on Boarding. *Emergency Department Overcrowding: High Impact Solutions* (Apr. 2008).

Chapter 4:

25   Stelfox, H.T. et al. *The American Journal of Medicine* 118 (2005): 1126-33.

26   Handel, D.A., R. Fu, M. Daya et al. "The use of scripting at triage and its impact on elopements." *Acad Emerg Med.* 17 (2010): 495-500.

27   Isaac, T. et al. "The Relationship Between Patients' Perception of Care and Measures of Hospital Quality and Safety." *Health Serv Res* 45, no. 4 (Aug. 2010): 1024-40. Epub May 28, 2010.

28   Terrell, K.M., C.S. Weaver, B.K. Giles, M.J. Ross. "ED patient falls and resulting injuries." *Emerg Nurs* 35, no. 2 (Apr. 2009): 89-92. Epub Jul. 10, 2008.

29 Meade, C.M. et al. "Effects of nursing rounds on patients' call light use, satisfaction, and safety." *American Journal of Nursing* 106, no. 9 (2006): 58-70.

30 GetWellNetwork Inc. "Improving heart failure outcomes through interactive patient care: the Sentara Virginia Beach general hospital experience." (Jun. 23, 2009).

31 Marty, H. et al. *Emerg Med Journal* (Mar. 2012). Epub ahead of print accessed May 15, 2012.

Chapter 7:

32 New South Wales Government. *2010 New South Wales Patient Health Survey.*

33 Frederickson, B.L., M.F. Losada. "Positive affect and the complex dynamics of human flourishing." *Am Psychol.* 60, no. 7 (Oct. 2005): 678-86.

Chapter 9:

34 HealthLeaders Media. *Volume, Flow, and Safety Issues in the ED* (May 2012).

35 *Emergency department visits involving nonmedical use of selected prescription drugs—United States, 2004 to 2008.* Centers for Disease Control and Prevention 59, no. 23 (Jun. 18, 2012): 705-9.

36 Millar, W.B. "Grounding frequent flyers, not abandoning them: drug seekers in the ED." *Ann Emerg Med.* 49, no. 4 (Apr. 2007): 481-6.

37   Nabb, M. et al. "Diagnosing drug-seeking behavior in an adult emergency department." *Emergency Medicine Australasia* 18 (2006): 138-42.

38   Baehren, D.F. et al. "A statewide prescription monitoring program affects emergency department prescribing behaviors." *Ann Emerg Med.* 56, no. 1 (Jul. 2010): 19-25.

Resources

Access additional resources at www.studergroup.com.

ABOUT STUDER GROUP:

Learn more about Studer Group by scanning the QR code with your mobile device or by visiting www.studergroup.com/about_studergroup/index.dot.

Studer Group® helps over 800 healthcare organizations in the U.S. and beyond achieve and sustain exceptional clinical, operational, and financial outcomes. As they face ever greater quality demands—HCAHPS, Core Measures, preventable readmissions, hospital-acquired conditions, and more—they engage us to help them create cultures of execution. Using our Evidence-Based Leadership℠ framework as the starting point, we hardwire processes that get them aligned, accountable, and agile so they can execute proven tactics quickly, consistently, and in the right sequence…and sustain the results over time. We also help them foster better integration with physicians and other service providers in order to create a smooth continuum of patient-centered care.

STUDER GROUP COACHING:

Learn more about Studer Group coaching by scanning the QR code with your mobile device or by visiting www.studergroup.com/coaching.

<u>Healthcare Organization Coaching</u>
As value-based purchasing changes the healthcare landscape forever, organizations need to execute quickly and consistently, achieve better outcomes across the board, and sustain improvements year after year. Studer Group's team of performance experts has hands-on experience in all aspects of achieving breakthrough results. They provide the strategic thinking, the Evidence-Based Leadership framework, the practical tactics, and the ongoing support to help our partners excel in this high-pressure environment. Our performance experts work with a variety of organizations, from academic medical centers to large healthcare systems to small rural hospitals.

<u>Emergency Department Coaching</u>
With public reporting of data coming in the future, healthcare organizations can no longer accept crowded Emergency Departments and long patient wait times. Our team of ED coach experts will partner with you to implement best practices, proven tools, and tactics using our Evidence-Based Leadership approach to improve results in the Emergency Department that stretch or impact across the entire organization. Key deliverables include improving flow, decreasing staff turnover, increasing employee, physician, and patient satisfaction, decreasing door-to-doctor times, reducing left

without being seen rates, increasing upfront cash collections, and increasing patient volumes and revenue.

Physician Integration & Partnership Coaching
Physician integration is critical to an organization's ability to run smoothly and efficiently. Studer Group coaches diagnose how aligned physicians are with your mission and goals, train you on how to effectively provide performance feedback, and help physicians develop the skills they need to prevent burnout. The goal is to help physicians become engaged, enthusiastic partners in the truest sense of the word—which optimizes HCAHPS results and creates a better continuum of high-quality patient care.

BOOKS: categorized by audience

Explore the Fire Starter Publishing website by scanning the QR code with your mobile device or by visiting www.firestarterpublishing.com.

Senior Leaders & Physicians
Leadership and Medicine—A book that makes sense of the complex challenges of healthcare and offers a wealth of practical advice to future generations, written by Floyd D. Loop, MD, former chief executive of the Cleveland Clinic (1989-2004).

Engaging Physicians: A Manual to Physician Partnership—A tactical and passionate roadmap for physician collaboration to generate organizational high performance, written by Stephen C. Beeson, MD.

Straight A Leadership: Alignment, Action, Accountability—A guide that will help you identify gaps in Alignment, Action, and Accountability, create a plan to fill them, and become a more resourceful, agile, high-performing organization, written by Quint Studer.

Excellence with an Edge: Practicing Medicine in a Competitive Environment—An insightful book that provides practical tools and techniques you need to know to have a solid grasp of the business side of making a living in healthcare, written by Michael T. Harris, MD.

Physicians
Practicing Excellence: A Physician's Manual to Exceptional Health Care—This book, written by Stephen C. Beeson, MD, is a brilliant guide to implementing physician leadership and behaviors that will create a high-performance workplace.

All Leaders
The Great Employee Handbook: Making Work and Life Better—This book is a valuable resource for employees at all levels who want to learn how to handle tough workplace situations—skills that normally come only from a lifetime of experience. *Wall Street Journal* bestselling author Quint Studer has pulled together the best insights gained from working with thousands of employees during his career.

Hey Cupcake! We Are ALL Leaders—Author Liz Jazwiec explains that we'll *all* eventually be called on to lead someone, whether it's a department, a shift, a project team, or a new employee. In her trademark slightly sarcastic (and hilarious) voice, she provides learned-the-hard-way insights that will benefit leaders in every industry and at every level.

The HCAHPS Handbook: Hardwire Your Hospital for Pay-for-Performance Success—A practical resource filled with actionable tips proven to help hospitals improve patient perception of care. Written by Quint Studer, Brian C. Robinson, and Karen Cook, RN.

Hardwiring Excellence—A *BusinessWeek* bestseller, this book is a road map to creating and sustaining a "Culture of Service and Operational Excellence" that drives bottom-line results. Written by Quint Studer.

Results That Last—A Wall Street Journal bestseller by Quint Studer that teaches leaders in every industry how to apply his tactics and strategies to their own organizations to build a corporate culture that consistently reaches and exceeds its goals.

Hardwiring Flow: Systems and Processes for Seamless Patient Care— Drs. Thom Mayer and Kirk Jensen delve into one of the most critical issues facing healthcare leaders today: patient flow.

Eat That Cookie!: Make Workplace Positivity Pay Off...For Individuals, Teams, and Organizations—Written by Liz Jazwiec, RN, this book is funny, inspiring, relatable, and is packed with realistic, down-to-earth tactics to infuse positivity into your culture.

"I'm Sorry to Hear That..." Real-Life Responses to Patients' 101 Most Common Complaints About Health Care—When you respond to a patient's complaint, you are responding to the patient's sense of helplessness and anxiety. The service recovery scripts offered in this book can help you recover a patient's confidence in you and your organization. Authored by Susan Keane Baker and Leslie Bank.

101 Answers to Questions Leaders Ask—By Quint Studer and Studer Group coaches, offers practical, prescriptive solutions to some of the many questions he's received from healthcare leaders around the country.

Over Our Heads: An Analogy on Healthcare, Good Intentions, and Unforeseen Consequences—This book, written by Rulon F. Stacey, PhD, FACHE, uses a grocery store analogy to illustrate how government intervention leads to economic crisis and eventually, collapse.

Nurse Leaders and Nurses
The Nurse Leader Handbook: The Art and Science of Nurse Leadership—By Studer Group senior nursing and physician leaders from across the country, is filled with knowledge that provides nurse leaders with a solid foundation for success. It also serves as a reference they can revisit again and again when they have questions or need a quick refresher course in a particular area of the job.

Inspired Nurse and *Inspired Journal*—By Rich Bluni, RN, helps maintain and recapture the inspiration nurses felt at the start of their journey with action-oriented "spiritual stretches" and stories that illuminate those sacred moments we all experience.

Emergency Department Team
Excellence in the Emergency Department—A book by Stephanie Baker, RN, CEN, MBA, is filled with proven, easy-to-implement, step-by-step instructions that will help you move your Emergency Department forward.

INSIGHTS FROM STUDER GROUP EXPERTS:

Access current and archived Insights by scanning the QR code with your mobile device or by visiting www.studergroup.com/thoughts/insights.dot.

Quick, to-the-point articles from founder Quint Studer and other Studer Group experts provide critical information and incisive commentary on hot industry issues.

SOFTWARE SOLUTIONS:

<u>Leader Evaluation Manager</u>™: <u>Results through Focus and Account-ability</u>—Organizations need a way to align goals for their leaders, create a sense of urgency around the most important ones, and hold leaders accountable for meeting their targets. Value-based purchasing, which forces you to improve faster and faster, makes this more critical than ever. Studer Group's Leader Evaluation Manager automates the goal setting and performance review process for all leaders, creating an aligned organization where everyone is striving for clear, measurable, weighted goals.

<u>Patient Call Manager: The Clinical Call System</u>SM—This agile, HIPAA-compliant system—designed to streamline the pre-visit and post-visit call process—allows you to provide a strong continuum of patient care and position your organization to greatly decrease preventable readmissions. It enables users to modify questions by patient risk groupings, focus in on key initiatives, and expand as imposed regulations grow.

To learn more, please visit
www.firestarterpublishing.com.

INSTITUTES:

To learn more about and register for upcoming Studer Group institutes, scan the QR code with your mobile device or visit www.studergroup.com/conferences_webinar/upcoming_institutes.dot.

<u>HCAHPS Summit</u>
Good HCAHPS performance is critical. In fact, it's the key that unlocks the door to improvement in all other areas impacted by value-based purchasing: process of care measures, preventable readmissions, HACs, and more. This intensive two-day institute immerses leaders in the behaviors and tactics proven to improve HCAHPS results and, ultimately, all quality measures. Each learning session is led by top industry experts and provides research-based tactics proven to impact each specific composite. You'll discover the cultural factors that hold employees accountable and accelerate your ability to provide the kind of transformative care organizations need to thrive in the Age of Quality.

<u>Taking You and Your Organization to the Next Level</u>
At this two-day institute, leaders learn tactics proven to help them quickly move results in the most critical areas: HCAHPS, Core Measures, preventable readmissions, hospital-acquired conditions, and more. They walk away with a clear action plan that yields measurable improvement within 90 days. Even more important, they learn how to implement these tactics in the context of our Evidence-Based Leadership framework so they can execute quickly and consistently and sustain the results over time.

Nuts and Bolts of Operational Excellence in the Emergency Department

Crowded Emergency Departments and long patient wait times are no longer acceptable, especially with public reporting of data in the near future. We can predict with great accuracy when lulls and peak times will be, and we know exactly how to improve flow and provide better quality care. This institute will reveal a few simple, hard-hitting tactics that solve the most pressing ED problems *and* create better clinical quality and patient perception of care throughout the entire hospital stay.

Practicing Excellence: Engaging Physicians to Execute System Performance

The changes mandated by health reform make it clear: There will surely be some sort of "marriage" between hospitals and physicians. Regardless of what form it takes, we must start laying the groundwork for a rewarding partnership *now*. Learn our comprehensive methodology for getting physicians aligned with, engaged in, and committed to your organization so that everyone is working together to provide the best possible clinical care, improve HCAHPS results, increase patient loyalty, and gain market share.

What's Right in Health Care®

One of the largest healthcare peer-to-peer learning conferences in the nation, What's Right in Health Care brings organizations together to share ideas that have been proven to make healthcare better. Thousands of leaders attend this institute every year to network with their peers, to hear top industry experts speak, and to learn tactical best practices that allow them to accelerate and sustain performance.

For information on Continuing Education Credits, visit www.studergroup.com/cmecredits.

About the Authors

Stephanie Baker, RN, CEN, MBA

Stephanie has over 25 years of clinical nursing and administrative experience in the areas of emergency, trauma, flight, and critical care medicine and proven results with her partners around the country.

As vice president of emergency services, Stephanie leads Studer Group's ED service line and oversees more than 1,000 Studer Group ED engagements and strategic partnerships. In addition to serving as national keynote speaker for Studer Group's two-day Excellence in the Emergency Department Institute, Stephanie is also the author of the best-selling book *Excellence in the Emergency Department: How to Get Results.*

As a frequent contributor to the *Journal of Emergency Nursing* *(JEN)*, readers voted her 2010 article on bedside shift report one of the "Top 25 hottest articles" of the year. She is also a frequent speaker at national industry professional associations, including her upcoming "Five Ways to Diagnose and Treat Your ED" presentation at the 2013 Emergency Nurses Association (ENA) Leadership Conference, and a popular presenter on a wide range of ED topics at organizations nationwide (www.StuderGroup.com/Speaking).

She is a past recipient of the prestigious "Tribute to Women in Industry" (TWIN) Award, a nine-time Studer Group Pillar Award winner, and the recipient of the prestigious Studer Group "Flame" Award. Stephanie's philosophy is "Sometimes we get only one chance." Her goal is to make a difference with every patient every time.

Regina Shupe, RN, MSN, CEN

With more than 25 years of experience in emergency, trauma, critical care, and clinical nursing and nursing leadership, Regina serves as an ED expert coach in the Emergency Department service line for Studer Group. She currently coaches Emergency Departments in large academic medical centers, community and rural hospitals, as well as more than 1,200 ED physicians in over 400 Emergency Departments via National EmCare.

A 2012 winner of Studer Group's Pillar Award for achieving excellent partner results in ED operations, service, and quality, Regina offers her partners exceptional depth and breadth of experience. Prior to joining Studer Group in 2008, she was director of emergency services at West Chester Medical Center in Cincinnati, OH, currently ranked in the 99th percentile for patient satisfaction with a door-to-doc time of just 16 minutes.

A certified emergency nurse (CEN) who is also LEAN-certified for healthcare, Regina is also a coauthor of *The Nurse Leader Handbook: The Art and Science of Nurse Leadership* and Studer Group's white paper *The Emergency Department: Front Door to Pay-for-Performance*. A national speaker at Studer Group's Excellence in the Emergency Department Institute, Regina also speaks at EDs nationwide on a wide range of topics. She is perhaps best known for her great sense of humor and results-driven approach. Visit www.StuderGroup. com/Speaking.

Dan Smith, MD, FACEP

In addition to serving as an international coach and speaker for Studer Group's Emergency Department service line, Dan Smith, MD, FACEP, has also practiced emergency medicine for 15 years in the Emergency Departments of Baptist Health System, San Antonio, TX, as an independent contractor with Emergency Physicians' Affiliates (EPA).

He has also served as director of EPA's patient experience team since 2007, quadrupling the group's patient satisfaction through leadership, analysis, intervention, and training of 60-plus ED physicians and mid-level providers, while maintaining his personal overall physician satisfaction at the 98th percentile in one large national patient satisfaction database for the last 20 consecutive quarters.

Since joining Studer Group in 2008, Dr. Smith has coached, mentored, and lectured at more than 100 healthcare organizations in the United States, Canada, and Australia. (For a list of popular ED presentations, please visit www.StuderGroup.com/Speaking.) Dr. Smith is a frequent speaker at Studer Group's national Excellence in the Emergency Department Institute, Practicing Excellence Institute, What's Right in Health Care® Conference, and has presented at conferences for several chapters of the American College of Emergency Physicians.

In addition to authoring Studer Group's Q&A on *How to Manage Drug-Seeking Patients in the Emergency Department* and *How to Improve Flow for High-Performing Emergency Departments*, Dr. Smith has shared his expertise in numerous Studer Group insights, ED webinars, and videos. He was awarded Studer Group's Pillar of Excellence Award in 2011.

A diplomate of the American Board of Emergency Medicine, Dr. Smith completed a residency in emergency medicine at William Beaumont Hospital in Royal Oak, MI, where he was chief resident and was awarded Emergency Medicine Resident of the Year in 1997-98. He completed medical school at Indiana University (IU) in 1995, where he was awarded the "Excellence in Emergency Medicine" certificate by the Society for Academic Emergency Medicine on behalf of IU. Dr. Smith's motto: "Slow and steady wins the race."

How to Order Additional Copies of

Advance Your Emergency Department
Leading in a New Era

Orders may be placed:

Online at:
www.firestarterpublishing.com

Scan the QR code with your mobile device to order through
the Fire Starter Publishing website.

By phone at: 866-354-3473

By mail at: Fire Starter Publishing
913 Gulf Breeze Parkway, Suite 6
Gulf Breeze, FL 32561

Share this book with your team—and save!
Advance Your Emergency Department is filled with valuable
information for staff members at every level. That's why we're
offering bulk discounts when you order multiple copies.
(The more you order, the more you save!)
For details, see www.firestarterpublishing.com.

Advance Your Emergency Department
is also available at www.amazon.com.